# Utopia
## The Psychology of a
## Cultural Fantasy

# Studies in Speculative Fiction, No. 5

## Robert Scholes, Series Editor

Alumni/Alumnae Professor of English
Brown University

## Other Titles in This Series

# Utopia
## The Psychology of a Cultural Fantasy

by
David Bleich

UMI RESEARCH PRESS
Ann Arbor, Michigan

Produced and distributed by
UMI Research Press
an imprint of
University Microfilms International
A Xerox Information Resources Company
Ann Arbor, Michigan 48106

Library of Congress Cataloging in Publication Data

**Bleich, David.**
    Utopia : the psychology of a cultural fantasy.

    (Studies in speculative fiction ; no. 5)
    "Revision of the author's thesis, New York University,
1970"—Verso t.p.
    Bibliography: p.
    Includes index.
    1. English fiction—History and criticism. 2. American
fiction—History and criticism. 3. Utopias in literature.
4. Fantasy in literature. 5. Psychoanalysis and literature.
I. Title. II. Series.
PR830.U7B54 1984    823'.8'09372       84-2537
ISBN 0-8357-1574-4

# Contents

# 1

# The Motivating Fantasy and the Study of Modern Utopias

It has long been the custom to understand cultural and historical phases by giving them a name—the Iron Age, the Age of Adventure, the Age of Reason, for example, and now, if one can really name one's own epoch, the Age of Anxiety. This practice creates a handy intellectual matrix which can both identify the age and coordinate its various aspects. As this brief list suggests, the approach of contemporary times brings names of decreasing tangibility and increasing complexity, names which are more and more rooted in subjective processes. The change in these names, moreover, reflects the increased subjectivity in our sense of the historical phases; more significantly, it reflects our growing awareness of subjective features of the world at large. It is now necessary to characterize not simply the cultural movements, but the continuum between these movements and the personal, emotional lives of the individuals activating these movements. Putting the issue in terms of the traditional disciplines of cultural investigation, it is now necessary to be able to shift systematically between the more patently emotional aspects of culture—biography and art—and the common ideological matters of organized civilization, the public or social sector.

Perhaps it is a mistake to hope for systematic theories in this connection. Perhaps a theory is too rigid a structure to apply to entities as variable and amorphous as emotions, especially on a scale as large as culture itself. Yet the notion of "theory," even in the most exact sciences, has taken on new aspects of flexibility, tentativity, and choice. In the not-so-exact social sciences, meanwhile, it has become possible, if the demand for rigor is not exaggerated, to gain intellectual access to areas heretofore deemed intractable and mysterious because of their emotional underpinnings. Such new modes of understanding, aiming to unite personal and societal issues, beginning at the end of the nineteenth century in psychoanalysis and pragmatism and continuing on into the present, suggest how to revise our traditional "naming" procedure through a new *principle of understanding* that accounts more regularly for the emotions involved in cultural life.

The principle is that a *motivating fantasy*[1] can be discovered as the common ground between the personal lives of cultural leaders, works of imagination read by the public in general, and more abstract intellectual commitments of the age. A fantasy is, perhaps, an operational definition of a feeling. It is a way of *naming the feeling in dynamic or behavioral terms* rather than in simple denotational terms like "love" or "fear" or "anxiety." The familiar masculine oedipal fantasy, for example, "I wish to kill father and marry mother," was the name psychoanalysis gave to the emotional correspondence between early childhood and certain phenomena in the larger institutions of civilization, such as the struggle for political power or the wish for heavenly salvation. These adult embodiments of the infantile emotions are generically viewed as *defenses*, acceptable ways of socializing the spontaneous thoughts and impulses of individuals. A motivating fantasy should be understood to exist in conjunction with a characteristic defense that depends upon the areas of life in which the fantasy is operating. The defense is recognizable by its role as a socially directed ordering principle, such as child's play, artistic form, law and order, religious ritual, or the habitual lifestyle of an individual. In order to perceive the fantasy by itself, it must be sifted out from its defensive context, which acts both as a means of expression for the fantasy and as a means of disguise, much like ordinary clothing behaves with respect to human sexuality. Our main aim is to assemble a cultural wardrobe of defenses and demonstrate that in a particular age or historical phase these are in fact garments variously worn by a thematically repeated emotional anatomy of the culture.

To say that a fantasy is a name is complicated enough to require review of how it was first presented psychoanalytically.[2] For a long time in early psychoanalytic practice, the concept of fantasy was not used. Patients, Freud believed, simply relived verbally certain traumatic events in their past, and gained insight into their current emotional paralyses by discovering the analogical relationship between painful childhood conditions and the adult malaise. It was soon observed that many of the traumatic childhood events reported by patients, usually involving precocious and perverse sexual experience with parents, *were not real*, but were invented by the patients and reported *as if real*. This led to the understanding that imaginary events—those created in fantasy by the patient —were in some important sense equally determinant of emotional life as real events.[3] Moreover, events created in fantasy bore a distinct relationship to the actual childhood history, such that the fantasy became an adult way of verbalizing the emotional dynamics of childhood. It became the adult's way of expressing—in sexual terms—what the child lacked the language for articulating, though the "sexual" feelings were nevertheless present in childhood. For example, the oedipal situations often reported by patients were thereby discovered to be oedipal *fantasies,* or, as was equally common, oedipal dreams. In this sense, the fantasy *names* the feeling of childhood. Psychoanalysis does not conceive of a small boy insidiously plotting murder of his father and secretly arranging for intercourse with his mother. This is simply adult language for the common childhood situation in which the boy senses interference from the father to his insistent need of his mother. The boy's actual fantasy will be that his father is just not there while his mother is always at his disposal, and this fantasy itself will be delimited in time in the sense that the boy will not always be entertaining it under normal circumstances. The fantasy thus characterizes the stage of the child's emotional development.

For girls, the oedipal fantasy is analogous but different in fundamental ways. It is not simply that a little girl wishes her mother out of the way in order to possess her father, though this behavior is common in girls of three to five years old. Rather, the little girl's identification with the mother must be of a fundamentally different sort than the boy's identification with the father in the following way: the little girl is going *back* to the parent from whom she separated as an infant, whereas the boy is identifying with a "new" parent, so to speak, one from whom he did not previously separate during the second developmental phase.

This fact is pertinent in this particular study because, as will become clear, the utopian fantasy will be understood as something peculiarly masculine, or gender-specific, and decidedly unfeminine, because of the imagery of Mother Earth or Mother Nature as perceived by all the (masculine) utopists being discussed. At various points in the discussion, we will take note of the masculine character of the utopian fantasy.

As organized research continued in psychoanalysis, the oedipal situation was found to be a culmination rather than the inception of the first phase of early child development. Technically, the genital-locomotor stage appears at the age of four or five, or at least at this age it is most easily discernable. Other developmental stages were seen to precede genital-locomotor behavior, so that in adulthood, different kinds of fantasies were discovered which represented these earlier childhood stages. Each of these stages, genital included, were found to center about the growing consciousness in the child of his or her own body, and especially of the parts which were consistently used and stimulated. Thus, the first stage concerned oral-sensory activity, which is characterized by the child's crying for food, getting it, crying, and getting it again; in each case his or her own oral activity seemed to bring on an oral stimulation via the breast or the bottle, and brought, in any case, the mother herself. Fantasies of adult life rooted in this stage usually concern everlasting allegiance to causes or institutions conceived of in feminine terms, such as Mother Country or Mother Church or Mother Nature, and perhaps Alma Mater, from whence eternal emotional nourishment is forthcoming. The next major stage, the anal-muscular phase, concerns elimination activity, because up until this time the child is not conscious of any control he or she may exercise over these functions. At this point, the child is taught to exercise such control, to retain and to eliminate only in a specific place, and the child develops a fascination with both process and products. From this stage adult fantasies of social control and political order are created, fantasies of forever collecting or forever eliminating some suitable commodity, the most common of which is money. Finally, at the genital-locomotor stage, the child becomes conscious of the erotic potential of the genital region, which in turn is linked with the child's social situation as he or she notices that there are two different sexes in the world, each with different genital equipment, and that he or she has different needs from different parents. The fantasy associated in adult life commonly revolves, for example, around love triangles which harbor conscious adult wishes to eliminate rivals.

After a relatively desexualized "latency" period, in which the problems of social adjustment to the peer group are confronted, the child reaches puberty and subsequent adolescence. These infantile emotional phases return powerfully in fantasy form and cause some turbulence until the individual can develop adult capacities strong enough to control them and put them to productive use. All along, however, the roots of adult identity have been forming the child's growing *ego*. This agency, in its capacities for conscious initiative, acquires its characteristic form with the onset of syntactical language, which from then on is the major tool of initiative, though other techniques are learned as well.[4] The ego learns to conceive first of bodily functions but then of the self as a whole as needing regulation with respect to everything that is not a part of this self. The ability to affect a compromise between the inner demands of the person and all that is "other" so that both inner and other are optimally satisfied is defined by the individual's relative strength in selfhood.

This regulatory function of the ego is generally viewed as a process of establishing characteristic *defenses,* or strategies of psychosocial self-management, many of which stay with the individual for life. The aggregate of these strategies in adulthood is seen by others as the person's *identity*. While the various fantasies a person entertains throughout life represent a rudimentary response to the awareness of the infantile sources of his or her feelings, the fantasies are less visible than the more common and more complex array of regulatory strategies which are embodied in the conscious life-choices the individual makes. These include vocation, choice of spouse, ambitions, geographical location, furniture, and other, more elaborate enterprises along these lines. These strategies not only control the main emotional constellation generated in childhood, but also aim to provide the optimum conditions for the expression of these emotions.

The regulatory strategies governing the creation of the adult identity are most easily discoverable, in the absence of the psychoanalytic situation, from the early domestic life of the individual; home is the first proving ground. Furthermore, because in the home the first "others" in the person's life establish his or her first external milieu, this domain offers the least developed set of management strategies, and hence the best place from which to infer the motivating fantasies which express the person's deepest emotional needs. For many public figures who inspired biographical study, the paucity of psychological knowledge on the part of the biographer led more to histories of the individual than to analytical presentations of their lives. Nevertheless, in many of these biographies, as well as in those by more psychologically oriented scholars, enough factual information is presented to get at least a rudimentarily plausible basis from which to infer the more germane psychological factors. Furthermore, almost all sensitively drawn biographies include much factual data about the social milieu of both parents and subject, so that the development of the subject's sense of self, identity, as well as motivating fantasies are both corroborated and given a new dimension.

This social dimension in classical psychoanalysis was of far less prominence than it is in contemporary psychoanalysis, which takes into account the idea that both society and social values play an instrumental role in the creation of the sense of self and the crystallization of early fantasy life. My principal source for this view is Erik Erikson's *Childhood and Society*.[5] This work, now almost 40 years old, is a high point in post-Freudian psychoanalysis, which having studied unconscious processes, now undertook to learn how these processes are relative to the individual's historical situation and how this situation determines a person's means of conscious self-regulation in response to his or her unconscious makeup. Study of societal processes in general were now asked to enlarge Freud's initial theory of human personality.

Erikson's main task lay in finding, in review of three technological societies and two nontechnological ones, the social "modalities" which can be said to recreate the infantile emotional stages (outlined above) of the general membership in the society. This involved study of the customary rather than the pathological in child-rearing, though deviant cases were frequently cited. Based on original psychoanalytic understanding of neurotic emotional habituation, the process of ordinary, and then of normative, habituation was suggested as the root of what we commonly call "national character," or, as Erikson prefers, "national identity." Where early psychoanalysis stressed the ontogenetic development of the infant, Erikson tries to fit the collectivity of these developments into a pattern of social mutuality between generations, as well as between tradition and the living population.

The result is that Erikson showed, in specific terms, how individual development and social values mutually interact. What is distinct in this system from both early psychoanalysis and the older conception of social functioning in general, is that now the fantasy lives of both the adult generation and the fantasies activating the local traditions are traced as tangible forces in the ontogenetic development of the child. Public fantasies—religious, political, legendary, or literary—are now seen as isolable in their own right, and, varying with the individual, instrumental in creating the psychological groundwork that is to form the personality of the child in his or her subsequent adult world. The key public fantasies of this world, in turn, form a generalization of the childhood fantasies of its leading figures and the mythologies of the general population. This is what Erikson means when he refers to Hitler's and Maxim Gorky's respective childhoods as "legends," which are projected in the adult generation of these men as the motivating fantasies of their societies at large. The emotional tribulations in the childhoods of one generation become public fantasy material for the childhoods of the next, and thus form a part of the new reality that these latter childhoods are to confront.

Insofar as these fantasies are names of emotional constellations, they constitute an earmark first of the individual's structure of defense and self-management, later of his or her personal and/or professional identity, and finally of the societal identity. The transformation of personal histories into legends and thence to social identities is obviously not new, for here we see the modern counterpart of ancient mythologies, which likewise made tales of origin, childhood, growth, and heroic identity emblematic of the emotional texture of the society as a whole. But the ordinary function of legends and mythologies asks us to look at their ordinary contexts, art and religion, both of which elaborate to the furthest limits the expressive potential of legends and mythologies. Understanding of religious commitment as social self-management has proven somewhat easier than similar understanding of art. Part of the reason for this is that specific forms of religion are more socially widespread than specific forms of art. Religious forms are usually much simpler than most artistic forms. Erikson, extending Freud's early speculations, suggests that the universality of religion, along with the great cross-cultural similarity of its forms, is traceable to the earliest mode of infantile development, the oral-sensory stage, when the infant puts itself at the complete disposal of the mother, offering all its "faith," so to speak. This situation is common to all human cultures because of the universal fact of human infantile helplessness. Variations in child-rearing become increasingly distinct cross-culturally in later stages of development, and these variations are reflected in the social rituals deriving from the confluence of the initial act of faith and the geographical and economic realities of the particular culture. What essentially simplifies our understanding is the lack of any acknowledged individual source for religious practice. Religion is *ipso facto* universal, originating at once from "God" and from all people. This absolute, totalistic character, along with the imperative form of its ethical teachings, mark its fantasy roots in the earliest and most absolutely demanding of infantile stages. The religious fantasy is humankind's earliest form of social response to the earliest individual psychological tasks.

While there are rudimentary similarities between artistic and religious fantasies, the larger perspective points up radical differences. Art invites individuality and identity; religion precludes it. In a sense, the artist is called upon by the public to donate his or her individuality to the common weal. "Reading Kafka," for example, is easily recognized as indulging in a distinct kind of emotional experience, where the experience is initially named by little more than the surname of the author. The wide area of choice we reserve for ourselves in art is defined as much by the artist as by the genre. "I'm not in the mood for Bergman," we would find ourselves saying, "I'd rather read Shaw." This wide variety of particular stamps, of moods, of emotional brand names is what wins our allegiance and assures our continued interest. Topically, at least, we can say that the commitment to art, whether by artist or audience, today calls for a *far more complex ego involvement* than the commitment to religion.

It is not surprising, therefore, that while psychoanalysis, early and late, was equally fascinated with both religion and art, its original orientation around unconscious processes and fantasy-life led to more fruitful understanding of religion than of art. Only recently has understanding commensurate with that of religion become more available. This understanding comes as part of the general shift of psychoanalytic attention in recent times to the phenomena of individuality and conscious functioning, to the problems posed to social existence by the conflicting lifestyles of persons and subgroups. Insofar as art has long cultivated a kind of passionate individuality, Freud's personal mystification at the power of particular formal configurations, whatever the medium, suggested that the problems that art posed for psychoanalysis as a theory of personality were not limited to aesthetic matters. Much as Erikson's suggestions opened the territory of society to psychoanalysis, Simon O. Lesser's 1957 book *Fiction and the Unconscious*[6] renders questions of artistic form of new importance to the general understanding of both personality and culture.

The key theoretical question has usually concerned the rules the artist follows in transforming rudimentary fantasies—his or her early ideas and impulses for a work—into the elaborate symbolic structure which seems to assume an identity of its own. It has often been observed by experts and dilettantes alike that "there are no new stories; only the same ones told over in different form." It is fair to conclude, then, that the artist takes an "old" story, or some slight variation of it, and by a special process makes it seem new in the reading. Lesser's study of this process led to a decisive analogy between artistic creation and human psychological functioning in general; namely, the rudimentary fantasies, the first ideas, and the "old story" can all be associated with the artist's— and ultimately, the reader's as well—basic emotional constellation developed in early childhood. The characteristic form of the work, its familiar identity, the means through which we recognize its individuality, can all be associated with the *defenses* of the artist, as they are created by his or her own identity and by the surrounding cultural forces, and these defenses are subsequently assumed by the reader as a handle for his or her own emotional fantasy response to the work. This interplay of fantasy and defense produces the artist's satisfaction with his work and the reader's enjoyment of it. The psychological rules of defensive dynamics, therefore, are behind the characteristic artistic transformation of fantasy material, behind the artist's *forming* of the work.

Just as defenses function in real life both as a disguise and an expressive vehicle for the individual's fundamental feelings, form in art does as much for the fantasy impulses of artist and reader. Form's various defensive capacities may be said to act like sexual foreplay, interposing a delay that miniaturizes the larger game of emotionally climactic action, and in this sense manage *and* increase the pleasure of this action. It is a distracting function that lends the art experience its element of excitement and emotional surprise and thus becomes an essential part of our entire pleasurable involvement with the work. Even though, we realize in adulthood, it was great fun to be an infant, it would not be so much fun to always behave like an infant again, to manifest all of infant-hood's uncritical abandon without a suitable context defined by the rules of adult life. The familiar complexity of adult life, not found in childhood, is due to the juxtaposition to our fantasy needs of the new necessity for defensive arrangements, arrangements which we generally view as offering adults a depth, a meaning, a profundity that childhood cannot have. In this light we can better understand the difference between the pleasure afforded by an elaborate, symbolically complex work like *The Brothers Karamazov* and a simpler tale like "Jack, the Giant-Killer," each of which may be viewed by a reader as having "the same" fantasy content. Defense in art—form—interposes a kind of realistic maze—be it social problems or simply adult vocabulary or play with the medium itself—between our consciousness and the passions we seek to recall or experience in vicarious ways.

The act of faith in art, the "willing suspension of disbelief," thus becomes considerably more complex than the act of faith in religion, as even suggested by the double negative with which Coleridge named the act. In confronting art we implicitly expect a far more complex defensive overlay than in confronting God, where we almost too openly seek an omnipotent parent to trust. In both religion and art we seek access to a completely new world—a world, as Lesser or as Erikson has indicated,[7] in which we accept both subjects with the holistic "basic trust" of the earliest infantile stage. But we demand in art additional material from later developmental stages which serves to recreate certain conditions of the real world—ego material—to hold our sense of self intact against the strong claims of the primary fantasy impulses. On the whole, we demand from art a more complicated tie with real life, a tie both more restricting and more permissive. The formal defenses we see in art are derived far more thoroughly from later life than the defenses we see in religion which are, familiarly enough, autocratic and invariant, like the infant.

Unlike religious faith, therefore, artistic faith can safeguard its own integrity. When we begin "disbelieving" a work of art, we throw it away, without a deep remorse of conscience and without wondering if art in general is worthless. We value art as much because of adult needs as infantile needs; this is plainly not the case with religion, the rejection of which seems to cause violent personal and social traumas. The integrity of art is continuously protected by the adult faculty of *taste,* through which, while we can acknowledge connections with infantile orality, we can also cultivate its mature discriminatory function, its manifest refinement of simple oral needs. Taste, furthermore, finds even wider horizons in the culture at large, in the sense that it often develops on a public scale—develops, that is, in response to other people's aesthetic choices as well as in individual response to artistic variety. The "religion of art," as it is often called, is thus more deeply rooted in the needs of the whole personality, infantile and adult, since the final arbiters of "good and evil" in art are people functioning in communities. In fact, because of the collective exercise of taste, the personal religious commitment to art is limited. Artistic value derives from altogether intrahuman needs.

Artistic formal structuring, insofar as it tries to accommodate the full range of these needs—childhood and adult, artist and audience—suggests how artistic value develops to begin with, and how it changes with history. A preliminary study of an audience's response to a particular work[8] suggests that the value accorded the work depends upon how strong it views the work's formal, defensive configuration to be. If the fantasy-content is perceived as too naked, as insufficiently decorated by culturally acceptable standards of artistic dress, the judgment will veer toward rejecting the work because it is not "artful" enough. While, on one hand, the perception of defensive strength obviously varies with the individual, more uniform standards of perception are also discernable, standards traceable to the cultural milieu and the historical period. In any given age, certain kinds of fantasy-content will prove more disturbing than others and demand a stronger defense if they are to be accepted as art. Understanding the fantasy and defense needs of people in a given culture could explain why, at one point, a given work did not catch on only to be later revered as a universal classic. Where one age perceives a weak defense and strong fantasy, subsequent ages could easily perceive an enjoyable balance. Conversely, works which enjoy immense popularity in one age only to be abandoned subsequently with disgust can also be taken as an index of the fantasy-defense needs of that particular epoch, where the loss of popularity tells how these needs changed on the large scale.

The close study of popularly received works of a certain age offers an inroad to cultural generalization as valid, if not more so, as a statistical survey of many works. Viewing formal configurations as defensive constructs lends a more inclusive value to these configurations, extending them from the traditional "aesthetic" address, which communicated mainly to other works of art, in one direction to the overall cultural mood, and in the other to the personal histories of those living in that mood. Viewing art as being motivated by a fantasy is what allows systematic linkage with nonartistic circles; viewing form as a specialized defense accounts for the differences between these areas *while remaining within the same theoretical framework*. This framework is based on the knowledge that no matter which way we turn, human motivation, individual and collective, must be at work in what we observe. This study attempts to extend what is presently understood of human motivation to areas where we know such motivation is present, but where we have as yet not seen how it is organized.

The Transition Period (1870 to 1914) in England and America affords a particularly workable arena for such a study. Although there is too much happening in this period to permit an exhaustive coordination of all major events, there is, reaching a climax in the period, the idea of utopia that can be viewed as expressing the period's unique historical identity. Exactly what the correspondence is between the idea and the more various drifts of the culture is to be discussed in this essay, but that there is a correspondence is clear from ordinary familiarity with the historical facts of the time. For this main idea of utopia, in any case, we seek to study the motivating cultural fantasy in three main areas.

First, we would like to get at some notion of a utopian fantasy in general and what specific cultural forms it characteristically found as it grew first from Plato, but more importantly, from More, who invented the word. Why did this new word catch on so pervasively, so that even now, in the absence of the traditional "utopia,"the word is more common than ever before? Why, in this light, was the Transition the height of utopian concerns as we know them; why, as Negley and Patrick show,[9] did more literary utopias appear in English between 1890 and 1950? How can we account for the unusually great popularity of the Bellamyite Nationalist Movement in America, or the success of the Fabian Society in forming the Labor Party in England? How, in short, does the utopian fantasy explain the sudden prominence of utopianism in the Transition, the diversity of forms it was able to take, only to fade out, as the twentieth century continued, to the status of a pure fantasy, an object of ridicule in the realm of serious cultural endeavor?

Second, in the biographical arena, two figures stand out as particularly germane embodiments of the utopian fantasy—H.G. Wells and Henry James. Of all those ordinarily associated with utopianism, perhaps none is more typically and thoroughly utopian than Wells, for he committed almost all of his professional life—the last four decades of it at any rate—to the promulgation and promotion of his "modern utopia." The texture of his life, the constellation of his social values, his spontaneous enthusiasm for science and technology, his almost uncontrollable impulse to create fantasies of new and strange worlds, his covert strain of deep nostalgia, and above all, his supervening drive to perfect nothing less than the whole world, combine to create what might best be called a utopian personality. James, meanwhile, represents what we would ordinarily view as the furthest thing from the utopian personality. He was one of the Transition Period's greatest novelists, but this role suggests its own utopian roots. In creating masterworks on both sides of the twentieth century, on both sides, symbolically, of the Atlantic Ocean, on both sides of the sexual divide, and on both sides of the "boundary" between objective and subjective, James sought to endow artistic form with an unprecedented range of totality. He tried, as Leon Edel has suggested,[10] to create his own "great good place" in the world of literary art. Emotionally, James was committed to creating in the world of artistic form what Wells aimed to create in the real world—a distinct condition of perfection and felicity.

The third area of inquiry is literature as a structured entity of common cultural possession. Two works, Wells's *A Modern Utopia* and James's *The Golden Bowl,* both published in 1905, fairly near the climax of the utopian upsurge, act out in textual form the fate of the utopian fantasy in the Transition. Wells's work, as we might expect, typifies the utopian novel, while James's work straddles the novel form typical of both centuries—in more than just a metaphoric sense: the first half is in the nineteenth-century idiom—realism—the second half in the twentieth—subjectivism. The form of the novel in general was the characteristic, popular art form of the day. Much as the film is today, it was the form in which one expected the widest range of imaginative treatment of contemporary issues—or any issues, for that matter. If, as proposed, the fantasies underlying each novel can today be taken as similar to one another, it is to the form, or to the individual author's reinterpretations of the novel's form, that any difference in the final value or significance of the two works could be traced.

Yet these two characteristic formal creations carry an even wider meaning. If they are rooted in both personal and public psychology of the age, the nuances and fluctuations inherent in the forms become emblematic, and the linguistic permanence in which they are represented becomes that much more important to the understanding of what was unstable and impermanent in the age. While often, in the past, artistic form has been taken in just such a sense, interpretation along these lines has been impressionistic, offering essentially isolated analogies, and implicitly finding more unified views of the culture unwieldy. In a sense, the critical aim has always been to find in artistic form a demonstration of the otherwise ineffable experience of an individual confronting large-scale civilized existence. But too often such interdisciplinary study has suffered a language gap, where the proponent of one discipline views the others as agents of its own perspective. The time spent in this essay reviewing psychoanalytic theory seeks to maintain a balance of integrity of both disciplines here in operation because new modes of understanding are inaccessible unless this is done. To enlarge the study of culture with psychological understanding of literature is really to propose rules for a new discipline, which in turn will find its own new objects of study.

In studying Transition utopianism as we are, trying to view it as an emotionally motivated entity, we seek means of unifying the emotional concerns of the age, of finding in the motivating fantasy a new *kind* of name for the age. A continuum might then be discernable between the aesthetic forms of the novels under scrutiny, the psychological patterns of their creators, and the emotional texture of the period.

# 2

# Utopia as a Cultural Fantasy

Fantasies, like stories and jokes, are never new. The feelings behind the fantasies have been repeatedly experienced since the human life began. The deepest pleasure we find in their expression grows from their familiarity rather than from their novelty. Ordinarily speaking, however, the notion of a "utopian fantasy" would have us locate its roots at the invention of the word in 1516. In part, it is true that utopianism as we now know it began when the word we use to conceive it entered the language. Yet insofar as a word is a symbol, and insofar as the founding work is a symbolic complex, the formal aspects of both word and work are, in our terms, the first modern adaptation of the utopian fantasy, the characteristically modern embodiment of feelings that must have existed in human beings from the beginning of civilization.

Most students of utopianism have acknowledged utopian notions in nonutopian forms. "The tendency to utopianize," Negley and Patrick write,

> is common to primitive and sophisticated men. Conceptions of Paradise, Arcadia, the Golden Age, the Island of the Blest, Gardens of Eden, and the Land of Cockaigne are reiterant in human thought. . . . Utopianism, explicit or implicit, is discoverable almost everywhere in literature.[1]

The search for utopian origins has led back almost 3,000 years to eighth-century B.C. Greece, where Arthur Morgan found Hesiod's early ruminations to be the "oldest clear expression of the Golden Age mythology in Greek literature,"[2] or where Negley and Patrick indicate that Lycurgus "drew up an ideal constitution and body of laws"[3] for Sparta. Although archetypal utopianism was obviously multiform—political, philosophical, or literary—a central determining feature of the impulse is soon suggested. It is that, whatever the context, the motivating feeling was one of *totality*. Whether the vision was bucolic, aureate, or diplomatic, these specific idioms were consistently enlarged to a scale of social holism, where all life was conceived of as being governed by the particular principle of the imagining mind.

The impulse to totality is somewhat clearer in the more marginally rational visions. The sun-state, for example, which Negley and Patrick see to be "reiterant in classical thought,"[4] is reminiscent of prehistoric sun-worship, where the sun has become the sufficient as well as the necessary condition for life. Most radical, probably, was Theopompus, who "described the land of Meropes, where all was gigantic and where there was a huge gulf full of red air which was neither light nor darkness."[5] The need to create a totality out of an immediate fetish, present even in modern utopianism when Bradford Peck, a department store owner, published *The World a Department Store* (1900), is a fact of psychic functioning. Under the stimulus of a lost fountain pen or a recalcitrant carburetor, infantile tantrums bring to the fore equally absurd wishes for the total transformation of society to a state where pens are unlosable and automobiles infallible. Even the earliest classical visions suggest that the utopian state of mind features this regressive aspect, in which distinctions between the partial malfunction and the total operation are dissolved, and life is seen, in clinical terms, as it is by the suckling child demanding his meal, whence his own "part" and the maternal whole are undifferentiable. The feelings of totality dissolve Gonzalo's familiar paradox: his commonwealth is the place where "no sovereignty"[6] and his own kingship are psychologically identical states.

The first forms of the utopian fantasy, then, appear in the social modality corresponding to the initial phase of individual development, the oral-sensory stage. They appear as the adult symbolization of the infant's search for a "basic trust" of his environment and his future, the success of which, as Erikson has suggested, ordinarily leads to the adult capacity to have hope.[7] As the Golden Age has in fact not arrived, the infantile search remains in adult life as a *wish*,[8] the wish for the return of the Golden Age of satiation, felicity, and inner equilibrium.

The onset of Christianity in the Western world effected the first major change of form in the utopian fantasy. The Golden Age was transformed into, on one hand, the Garden of Eden, and on the other, the promise of Heaven on Earth to be brought by the returning savior and his millenarian kingdom. Both the social modality of the Christian fantasy and its actual content suggest its affective identity with the older Golden Age of fantasy. Socially, Christianity made its appeal to all human beings, stressing the commonality of human destiny and the universality of the need to trust and to have faith. It was organized as a social institution, which, for many centuries, was subordinate to no other institution; supervised the ultimate processes of birth, mating, and death; and decreed the cosmology of the entire universe and its own "infallibility." The content of the fantasy, meanwhile, offered, in addition to the transcendant, omnipotent god, a fleshly effigy who had personal charge of one's destiny once the act of faith is rendered. The humanized masculine god would personally see to it that his "children" are "saved" and that ultimately all would be united in a single community of eternal bliss. It is not difficult to understand why this unified and purportedly universal cosmology superseded the various and transient cosmologies of the pagan eras. Christianity made more sense and offered more hope. It is as if the old wish came a step closer to fulfillment, while the new social form seemed to open new modes of rationality and social order.

The importance of the Christian fantasy in the present context is that it informed the milieu that gave birth to the most modern form of the utopian fantasy. And it did so in more ways than have been generally apparent. J.H. Hexter, for example, is unequivocal in asserting the importance of the fact that in 1515 More "did not know there was such a man as Martin Luther."[9] The impression is thus created that because "there could have been nothing further from Thomas More's mind"[10] than the oncoming cataclysm in Christianity, his "historical milieu" cannot possibly be related to this event, and that *Utopia* is in any case independent of it. While this may be true technically, it tends to limit understanding of the larger cultural framework that produced the work. For both before and during More's pre-*Utopia* lifetime, Christian ferment in England and on the Continent could not be only coincidentally analogous to the Lutheran revolution. Nor could More's final opposition to Henry VIII, buttressed as it was by his own opposition to Luther, be viewed as psychologically independent of his earlier hesitation to serve Henry, which itself was a major factor in the creation of *Utopia*. The spirit of the work, in short, is inescapably informed by More's own struggle to define the role of Christianity as a social and political force, and how can this struggle be seen as independent of the movement toward Reformation whether or not More knew about Luther? In this age, the Christian fantasy underwent a new test of its efficacy, and *Utopia* was one of the instances of the test.

Whatever the relationship between *Utopia* and the Reformation, however, they are both culminations as well as beginnings. The climactic test, as is suggested in Norman Cohn's work, *The Pursuit of the Millenium* (1957), had been brewing in Europe for a long time, and during this time fantasy analogues between England and the Continent are discoverable, although the main activity did center in north central Europe. While, on the major social scale, the Christian fantasy was firmly anchored in the ecclesiastical machinery until about the eleventh century, the fantasy in some small contexts gradually took on a somewhat different form that operated beyond the entrenched social structure of the Church. In this translated, more peripheral realm, the Christian fantasy became the millenarian fantasy, which, while embodying all the major elements of the "mother" fantasy, allots different stresses to different parts and in this way acts out the latent unrest and perhaps the growing inadequacy of the original fantasy.

The elements of this splinter fantasy, so to speak, like the more dominant ones, are also hardly new. The main Christian statement of it appears in Revelation, but Cohn traces "the central phantasy of revolutionary eschatology"[11] further, back to the Book of Daniel, composed about 65 B.C.

The world is dominated by an evil, tyrannous power of boundless destructiveness—a power moreover which is imagined not as simply human but as demonic. The tyranny of that power will become more and more outrageous, the sufferings of its victims more and more intolerable —until suddenly the hour will strike when the Saints of God are able to rise up and overthrow it. Then the Saints themselves, the chosen, holy people who hitherto have groaned under the oppressor's heel, shall in their turn inherit the dominion over the whole earth. This will be the culmination of history; the Kingdom of the Saints will not only surpass in glory all previous kingdoms, it will have no successors.[12]

This fantasy was largely dormant in Europe after it arrived, apparently in the second century. But increasing social turbulence in the eleventh century, Cohn suggests, began a long period of its activation, culminating in a series of attempted millenarian revolutions. The attempt to realize the fantasy disclosed its implicit wish for a single leader to mobilize the collective impulse, an individual to rally the hungry, suffering masses and yet deriving his own identity from them. Thus, the millenarian prophet overtook the key element of the original Christian fantasy: it was not God, but the *son* of God who is to be the savior. As a son, his identification with the "children" of God—the people themselves —took on a new power. The millenarian prophet extracted this latent power from the established religious fantasy and aimed for immediate realization. The psychological function of the prophet in the minds of his public was to activate the universal wish for total union with the infinite and *to embody the fulfillment of the wish,* the same wish of the earliest classical "utopists." A new and determining element was thereby added both to the classical fantasies and the dominant Christian fantasy: *the age-old wish is now a real possibility, indeed, a probability, and yes, a certainty.* Reality itself was now presumed subordinate to the authority of the wish. While there were always stories about the coming Kingdom of God, this was a major attempt actually to establish it.

Significantly, the millenarian fantasy, unlike the original Christian fantasy, was more than the psychological replacement of the weaker by the stronger; the weaker Golden Age fantasy, rather, was assimilated by and put into the service of the stronger. Cohn notes that in 1270, Jean de Meun's *Roman de la Rose* presents "a description of the Golden Age and the decline therefrom,"[13] describing an egalitarian State of Nature "for the first time since Antiquity."[14] Moreover, "no other vernacular work in the whole medieval literature was so popular."[15] Gradually, as this vision was publicly diffused, it was removed from its context in the past and reprojected into the future. Thus, by the end of the fourteenth century, the millenarian prophet

tried to call the equalitarian State of Nature out of the depths of the past and to present it as an attainable ideal. . . . The Millenium could now be imagined as a recreation of that lost Golden Age which had known nothing of social classes or of private property. During the great social upheavals which accompanied the close of the Middle Ages various extremist groups were inspired by the conviction that at any moment the egalitarian, communistic Millenium would be established by the direct intervention of God.[16]

Thus, merging the ancient and "modern" myths, both informed by the primary oral fantasy, and imbuing the new product with the certainty of immediate realization through the workings of a tangible human savior, the millenarian fantasy was able to gain an important foothold in the popular mind of the later Middle Ages.

While the Golden Age, Christian, and millenarian myths are driven by the same fantasy of infantile symbiosis, the wild violence of the latter myth in its drive for realization works out the main outward feature of its characteristic psychology: its adolescent structure. Often, the violence was directed against members of the established church, those priests called "Father" by the laity.[17] Yet more often, and more familiarly, it was the Jews, the patriarchal-looking figures that actually were the ancestors of Christianity, who caught the wrath of the fulminating chiliasts. The official pretext for violence against Jews was the desire for revenge growing from the conviction that the Jews murdered Christian children for their blood. Even further, Cohn includes a medieval engraving showing sadistic Jews gathered around an innocent Christian boy, sticking long pins into him and poised over his bleeding groin with a long knife. The Jews were thus imagined as castrating fathers, who, in this role as well as in the role of the final cause of the Black Death, were seen to be at the heart of the universal tyranny that was about to be overthrown. On the defensive stage of social realization, the specifically masculine oedipal fantasy appears: "father" will be removed by the saving son in order to recapture "mother" earth for the children of humanity.

It is in the period of masculine adolescence, we remember, when the oedipal—the masculine genital fantasy—and the earlier infantile phases re-emerge in the service of the newly acquired *real* sexual potency. In the young man, adolescence is when rebellion gets its first teeth, its first capacity for real violence in the family. Among his peers, the rebellious spirit of the adolescent youth gains a special importance in that he becomes at once a leader of men whose authority rests not on his distance from his followers but on his identity with them. Familiarly enough, the adolescent leaders of gangs "rebelling" against society display an especially wild zeal and energy. When the Christian fantasy was translated into the millenarian fantasy, thereby acquiring the imagined drive for realization, it rejected its traditional adult patriarchal defense—the institution of Church and clerics. Instead, it took on a still masculine, but now adolescent defense—the millenarian prophet, acting as the big brother who was going to kill father and save all the children from his castrating wrath and establish the nurturing bliss of millenarian totality.

Cohn, via the scheme of regression to adolescence, likens the millenarian fury to the recent catastrophe in Fascist Germany, even justifies his study as, in part, an attempt to discover historical roots of the perverse vision of the Thousand Year Reich. Similarly, Erikson views Hitler as

> the adolescent who refused to become a father by any connotation, or, for that matter, a kaiser or a president. He did not repeat Napoleon's error. He was the Fuhrer: a glorified older brother, who took over prerogatives of the fathers without overidentifying with them: calling his father "old while still a child," he reserved for himself the new position of the one who remains young in possession of supreme power. He was the unbroken adolescent . . . a gang leader who kept the boys together by demanding their admiration, by creating terror, and by shrewdly involving them in crimes from which there was no way back. And he was a ruthless exploiter of parental failures.[18]

It seems likely that the emergence of such intractably violent adolescent behaviors is correlatable with a crisis in social identity. Certainly this was the case in Germany, whose national identity had been in doubt and dispute even long before the Versailles Treaty. At the end of the Middle Ages, a similar identity crisis seems to have been gathering force. The arrival of the Golden Age myth from antiquity was only a symptom of the great cultural renaissance taking shape in southern Europe and gradually making its way north. The discovery of classical culture was a distinct threat to the prevailing ecclesiastical cosmology. It makes sense that a society losing the sense of its mature stability will in some sector adopt the psychic strategies of the search for identity in adolescence, and express in the violence of this stage the much deeper anxiety released by the loss of or damage to the patriarchal institutions which originally created in it the sense of "basic trust"—or religious faith.

Therefore, while the actual rebellion in Christianity did not come until Luther, it is clear that rebellion was in the air, as well as in the periphery of society, long before Luther. It is in these marginal movements, moreover, where the emotional roots of the main rebellion are most clearly discernable. For it is there, as if in symbolic form, that the drama of the loss and attempted recapture of religious identity is acted out in full psychological regalia, marked, Cohn well documents, by the characteristic social and sexual anarchy of the uncontrolled release of unconscious wishes. Accordingly, the complex of millenarian activity "appeared only when an organised insurrection of a decidedly realistic kind was already under way."[19] The analogy to the ongoing insurrection represented a sympathetic resonance of the overall threat to social identity; but the hysterical exaggeration of the analogy represented the return to the adolescent implementation of infantile autocracy.

Viewing the situation in terms of its fantasy elements, therefore, reveals distinct connections between the crisis in Christianity and the day of utopia. Quite some time ago, in fact, Karl Mannheim wrote that the "first form of the utopian mentality" is to be found in the "orgiastic chiliasm of the anabaptists":

Longings which up to that time had been unattached to a specific goal or concentrated upon other-worldly objectives suddenly took on a mundane complexion. They were now felt to be realizable—here and now—and infused social conduct with a singular zeal. . . . Orgiastic energies and ecstatic outbursts began to operate in a worldly setting, and tensions, previously transcending day to day life, became explosive agents within it. The impossible gives birth to the possible, and the absolute interferes with the world and conditions actual events. This fundamental and most radical form of the modern utopia was fashioned out of a singular material. It corresponded to the spiritual fermentation and physical excitement of the peasants of the stratum living closest to the earth. It was at the same time robustly material and highly spiritual.[20]

Cohn notes that Thomas Muntzer, whose activity Mannheim has in mind in this connection, "first broke away from Catholic orthodoxy as a follower of Luther."[21] Thus, Cohn's citation of Muntzer as the end point of medieval millenarianism and Mannheim's citation of him as the beginning of modern utopianism neatly coincide. Even without recourse to the fantasy motivating advanced millenarianism, its inner identity with utopianism is clear. In almost every instance of modern utopianism, one finds the "birth of the possible from the impossible," one finds a single utopist trying to bring it about, one finds the desire to transform the whole of society here and now, and one finds, above all, a strange excess of excitement and necessity governing the entire presentation. The notion of the fantasy lends the similarity, on the one hand, a conceptual unity, but more importantly, a firm grounding in the practical understanding of human development. The wish for the immediate realization of the "impossible" is the impulse to deny that self (people, peasants) and object (the nourishing land)—infant and mother—are in fact two different entities. It is the wish to restore the sense of uninterrupted bliss that comes of their original unity in the "State of Nature." The machinery used to activate this wish—its social forms—is the adolescent system of the charismatic, overzealous, overviolent big brother—the projection of the uncertain popular ego—doing away once and for all with the castrating father and thus restoring possession of "mother" earth—the land, the society, food, everything that sustains life.

The fantasy, finally, permits us to move across the channel into England and to sift out what is specifically utopian while still accounting for the different social milieu, which, in England, was marked by significantly less public violence than on the Continent. A good prototype of what was subsequently to become the characteristic Anglo-Saxon utopianism is the Peasant's Revolt of 1381, for while, as Cohn shows, millenarian fantasies accompanied this revolt, they appear in distinctly attenuated form compared to the continental fantasies. On the real, social level, vast economic inequity was the order of the day, mass discontent genuinely justified, and some kind of insurrection with limited social and political aims was both demanded and popularly desired. While, in the main, the insurrection was indeed so limited, the peripheral activities of the quasi-legendary John Ball, who promulgated the revolt "as part of a great eschatological drama,''[22] unquestionably imbued the revolt with much of its energizing passion. He purportedly delivered sermons citing the universal human ancestry of Adam and Eve and the consequent necessity to right the prevailing wrongs by making "all things . . . in common," and "all of us . . . of one condition."[23] Cohn tentatively suggests that "the burning of the palace of the Savoy and the destruction of all its treasure by Londoners who would take nothing whatsoever for themselves"[24] are the kinds of acts motivated by the implicit sense of eschatological purpose rather than by revolutionary expediency.

Nevertheless, these acts are "by-products" of the main movement. And this is the feature that distinguishes Anglo-Saxon utopianism from Continental. In the overall historical context, *the English were able to keep their utopian impulses in the manageable arenas of legality—and literature. This ability to control utopianism, moreover, is what has made utopianism what it is commonly understood to be today, an area of dream, of speculation, and of benevolent social ambition.* The violence at the heart of the utopian fantasy is translated in the English tradition into the familiar utopian sense of urgency, the feeling of necessity, and its implicit warning that unless utopian visions are realized, all will be lost. Victor Dupont has written that

> Pour cette quête infatigable [the utopian quest], le groupe anglo-saxon semble avoir été particulièrement désigné par les éléments de son tempérament composite. L'imagination poétique n'a jamais cessé de se manifester dans sa littérature, côte à côte avec le sens practique, et l'amour de l'ideal avec l'appréciation de realités concrètes.[25]

It seems eminently true that as early as the Peasant's Revolt, the "appreciation of concrete realities" was distinctly in force as part of the English national identity. It is a striking fact of history that, as J.L. Talmon has observed,

> Legality has entered into the English subconscious, into the English blood. It is quite hopeless to rely on the English to make a real revolution.[26]

For no other country in Europe has seen as little revolutionary violence as England. Perhaps, in fact, the relatively peaceful evolution toward democracy in English government can be partially explained by the siphoning off, through the utopian tradition, of truly aggressive, destructive, revolutionary impulses. In English society the public handling of ideas and literature proved adequate to contain the violent utopian fantasy for a long time; whereas, in Germany, even as far back as the Middle Ages, the fantasy forced its way through to social reality, culminating, as Cohn persuasively suggests, in the apocalyptic hysteria of the Thousand Year Reich.

Much as English utopianism can be now seen as a "legal," socially tractable form of German millenarianism, Thomas More can be understood as a civilized, better socialized form of Thomas Muntzer. While More died defending Catholic orthodoxy—the One True Church—Muntzer died defending millenarian orthodoxy—the League of the Elect. Both men, from remarkably similar viewpoints, died opposing partial reforms of the Christian world view, each demanding an analogous kind of totality. That is, while Muntzer wanted to throw out the old entirely, More wanted to keep the old entirely. The decisive difference between the two men was that More's "utopian" impulses to erect an entirely new order—implicit, by the way, in his subsequent dogmatic refusal to change the old—were confined to the literary sphere, *Utopia,* and thus within the rules of social decorum, while Muntzer actually tried to do the job in reality and thereby disclosed the weakness of his adolescent ideology. Both men, in short, were motivated by the *same fantasy* and were troubled by analogous crises of identity. But More, owing to features common to his personality and his society, expressed it in terms of traditional adult behaviors and thereby gained sainthood; Muntzer remains in the gallery of historical demons.

The ambivalent tonus of More's lifetime—his continuing struggle to balance orthodoxy and secular public life—is recognizable as an adolescent struggle to "find himself" and probably finds its beginnings during his actual adolescence when he spent two extremely pleasant years in the household of John Morton, Archbishop of Canterbury. It is probably during this period, under the kindly influence of Morton, that fantasy elements of reform and total change first crystallized within him, along with the corresponding principles of social decorum offered him by both Archbishop Morton and the society at large. It seems that his stay in this household, however, was not long enough, for throughout his lifetime More was torn between the real-world values of his father, who encouraged him to enter the legal profession, and the values of the cloister, with its emphasis on private learning, literature, and faith. As is well known, his adult life started in his father's idiom, as he entered the service, after long hesitation, of Henry VIII, all the while harboring misgivings about what he was doing and longings to return to scholarship and study. "He had no love for the profession imposed upon him," writes John Anthony Scott, "and he followed the paternal footsteps with reluctance."[27] But as is much better known and much more significant, his life ended up in the "idiom" of Cardinal Morton, opposing with unequivocal firmness the rash of heresy cropping up all about him, and finally in the court of the same king he formerly served. His opposition to the king can now be viewed as the climactic act of the long festering spirit of rebellion against his father, as in this ultimate act of self-sacrifice, the "father" segment of his lifetime, is finally abjured while his "real" self, so to speak, is defined in the machinery of its own destruction. One suspects that although self-sacrifice was in More's time a *bona fide* adult value in his faith and his society, the violence implicit in it is traceable to the adolescent *needs* for power and violence combined with the imperative to repress them during his adolescence. It thus remained within him, emerged early in the fanta-

formed society, continued its attrition in More's subsequent life-... ultimately appeared in its most naked and tragic form as a "saint-...ut deadly opposition to the king.

Christian Humanism was the fabric of values from which this single value grew. Its topical texture, like that of martyrdom, seems indisputably laudable: it was an attempt to unite traditional values with newly acquired values. In part, no doubt, More's commitment to Humanism was secular in the modern sense. But judging from the emotional structure of More's adult life, the humanist impulse became allied with his repressed commitment to orthodoxy in opposition to the brutality and extravagant cruelty of public, political life with all its vicious infighting, intrigue, and foreign wars. *Utopia,* insofar as one of its major themes (if not the major theme) is the inherent opposition of the inner contemplative life and the outer public life of "philosophy and kings," and insofar as it is itself an act of literature and learning, seems clearly an act of Humanist-Christian opposition to the entire system of public real-life problems that More, in the service of his father's values, reluctantly joined. It is significant in this connection that in Utopia, while "each is brought up in his father's craft, . . . if anyone is attracted to another occupation, he is transformed by adoption to a family pursuing that craft for which he has a liking," and "care is taken not only by his father but by authorities"[28] that the youth is well placed. The inescapable good sense and good will of this custom, like the benevolence and felicity of all Utopia in particular, and of Christian Humanism in general, is a rational, sublimated resolution of the inner conflict More struggled with for a lifetime.

The articulation of the original utopian vision, the act of creating the work, became the cornerstone of his identity as a humanist scholar in his own time and as an author in subsequent history. Death came to him through his commitment to the public world, but his life was defined by what he imagined and what he wrote. Accordingly, insofar as the form of a literary work is a social management of a subjective fantasy, the formalism of *Utopia,* by now deemed a hallmark of More's existence, acts out the adaptive process that operated in his life. The two books of the work correspond to the two forces battling within him. The first book, simply enough, moves in the world of reality, the "high price of food," "this wretched need and poverty," the "ill timed luxury,"[29] "dives, brothels, . . . crooked games of chance," "the pursuits of war,"[30] the execution of thieves, the unjust laws—in short, the prevailing social degeneracy and chaos. In this situation shouldn't the wise, the philosophers, advise the king on what is right and just? No, says More to Raphael, "there is no room for philosophy with rulers."[31] This, of course, is the disillusioned and frustrated political More now about to serve the king, hiding another More inside, who was perhaps always in the service of John Morton, a More who left his "home" only against his better judgment.

This inner More appears in Book I actually in the home of Cardinal Morton, in the form of his famous protagonist, the "speaker of nonsense." In this "play within a play" the old intimate scene is recreated, whence realistic grievances are presented to the original hero of More's adolescence. Raphael's antagonist is a "layman, learned in the laws of your country,"[32] who after hearing Raphael out, promises to "demolish and destroy all your arguments,"[33] but is promptly restrained by the Cardinal, put off until "the next meeting"[34] which, significantly enough, never appears in the work. The structure of More's inner reality is clear. A kind of tribunal is set up, where the misery of the public weal, decried by the enlightened but fictitious alter ego of the now grown More, is presented to the opposed emblems of More's crystallizing identity, the Cardinal and his father. The aggressiveness of the latter, framed in the most extreme terms—the threat to "demolish and destroy *all*" of Raphael's views—is duly overcome, with equal finality, by the humane Christian hero, the Cardinal. In the real world, nevertheless, there remains "no room" for philosophy in the counsel of kings. This is the unfortunate truth.

There is room, however, in Book II for the speaker of nonsense, the grieving and frustrated member of society, to "report" the grounds of his discontent, and thus for the inner Christian Humanist to create in the first utopian fantasy the lost world that was incompletely formed in the home of Cardinal Morton. While on one hand the "new world," which Hythlodeus left behind so that he may tell of it, is the purported artistic disguise of the work's spirit of social rebellion, it is, on the other hand, the vision of the world More left behind when he entered the political merry-go-round in Henry's court, the world of art, letters, and faith. For him, the new world discovered across the ocean was not the real new world; the real discovery was the private, subjective learning and spiritual commitment that was *his own personal discovery* during his happy adolescent years. The appearance of the "new world" as part of the work's formal structure partakes of a crucial emotional ambivalence the term assumed during that age. In fantasy, the two kinds of new worlds—the geographical and the cultural—appear as the single occasion for a regressive wish that a general overturning of the present social turbulence will somehow remove all the anxiety the two real "new worlds" provoke. Obviously, it was not a new world that was discovered, but the other half of the old one. The "error" implicit in the term itself expresses the wish that a new world is really in the offing, and as More's work amply expresses, that a *new life* is likewise imminent. More's usage of the term, alongside the fiction that Hythlodeus actually travelled with one of the discoverers of the new world, shows the confluence in *Utopia* of the crisis in his own identity and the likewise "adolescent" crisis of identity that his culture was then undergoing.

The emotional constellation that the millenarians expressed in mob action, More expressed in legal, literary form. In either case, the motivating fantasy is the same—the wish for the complete overturn of the old order, for the dissolution of all boundaries, for total "equality." The defense, or adaptive form, though operating in different media, is metaphysically and emotionally the same —the adolescent posture of an intermediate figure intervening, committing the violent act of rebellion, and bringing, in the name of all human beings, social and personal salvation. It seems clear that the emotional equivalence of utopianism and millenarianism grows from the condition of major change in the prevailing cultural identity, change that threatens to do away with values from which the collectivity of individuals had, in youth, wrought their own identities. Utopia, in a sense, is the civilized response to the uncertain prospects of the formation of new cultural identities.

We say a civilized response, but nevertheless an adolescent one, for motivating the incipiently mature adolescent sense of real possibility is the infantile wish for immediate totality. This wish is never completely absent from adult life, but usually it acquires an adult—more containing and realistic—context. Thus, when perfection is reached in adult life, it is in a severely limited context, and when universality is achieved, it is only for a limited number of aims. The overall image of utopianism after More, in any case, retains the characteristic adolescent ambivalence between the mature and the infantile, between its civilized intentions—its anticipations of real possibilities in a literary format—and its motivating energies—its origins as an impulsive, anxious response to an imminent transformation of cultural identity. The important fact about this ambivalence, throughout the modern history of utopianism, is that *it is never really resolved,* for resolution in favor of either of its directions seems to imply the negation of its program. If resolved in the "real" direction, it brings chaos and destruction; if resolved in the literary direction, it becomes art; if a compromise is sought, it becomes politics as usual. This may explain why modern history is replete with "utopias" and utopian plans, often with serious commitments from major figures of the culture, without any of these utopian enterprises ever having gained the social, intellectual, or literary longevity, the condition of continuing relevance, achieved by other cultural enterprises of comparable ethical and emotional magnitude.

Utopianism has always been supported by arguments in the form of Frank E. Manuel's observation that "to attack utopias is about as meaningful as to denounce dreaming,"[35] that these "waking fantasies"[36] are expressive of central human impulses. In the present context, by and large, such arguments are borne out. Yet implicit in this argument is the further consideration that, as is herein suggested, the utopian dream or fantasy has never been able to acquire an identity more commensurate with mature consciousness and that it remains, like a dream, as a kind of unconscious reminder to civilization of its deepest, most irrational, most nostalgic, and most violent urgings. The puzzling aspect of this situation is not so much that utopianism is a dream or wish, but that its various forms of public presentation, the most revered domains of cultural enterprise, the ever present sense of possibility and genuine hope, the inherent civility, legality, and kindness, all fail to resolve the tension between the cultural fantasy and the demands of culture. Worse, failure seems to be the result of these same civil forms of cultural action, so that the whole utopian complex of ideas paradoxically implies its own dissolution and acts in a grotesque paradigm of the psychological defense that both invited, and enabled More to withstand, his own tortured end. It is noteworthy that this defense, intellectuality, has proved to be such a disappointment.

# 3

# The Paralysis of Utopian Intellectuality

There have always been intellectuals, just as there have always been fantasies. But it is easier to argue that fantasies have undergone essentially no change in their characteristic mode of functioning—an affective mode—than it is to argue that intellectuals have similarly retained an original mode. The intellectual moves in the world of consciousness. It is this world, rather than the biological Ur-world of unconsciousness, that has done all the changing in history. Consciousness can be viewed as responsible for changes in social form, where unconsciousness only informs consciousness of the need for possible active articulation of the response. Viewing the history of utopia from the context of the history of intellectual life thus suggests the likelihood of finding a major qualitative change, a distinct quantum jump in traditional intellectual categories. Perhaps the best evidence for such a change is the fact that "utopia," a new word—and hence, a new concept—was donated not only to the English language, but to all the world's major languages. This word is the first social translation of utopian feelings in their modern form, and it signals the contemporaneity of the particular ideational complex it represents. Above all, however, it furnishes a first clue to the problem of intellectuality as it functions as a promoter of the utopian fantasy.

Somewhere in the multiplicity of material between the title and the text of *Utopia,* there is a poem written by the "poet laureate" of Utopia as a kind of miniature fantasy of what the land of Utopia thinks of its own name and status in Western civilization.

> The ancients called me Utopia or Nowhere because of my isolation. At present, however, I am a rival of Plato's republic, perhaps even a victor over it. The reason is that what he has delineated in words, I alone have exhibited in men and resources and laws of surpassing excellence. Deservedly ought I to be called by the name of Eutopia or Happy Land.[1]

Although both More and his work are usually appreciated in terms of their modesty and humility, this relatively undiscussed poem opens complications. The usual critical reference to the poem stops at noting the pun in "Utopia," a pun that is implicit in the way the word is used to begin with. The poem suggests, however, that Eutopia as a kind of secret meaning of Utopia, is also a "rival" and a "victor" over its own principal precursor; even more significantly, it asserts its—the work's—rivalry and victory. This fantasy content of the poem recreates the larger fantasy of utopia in general. The formal defense of the poem's fantasy is the sense or the terms of its "victory." The old Utopia was nowhere, and Plato's republic was only in words, but "I alone" embodies "men, resources, and laws of surpassing excellence." What makes the Happy Land truly happy is that it conceives of itself as *real*, while the old Utopia was isolated in words. This new work, *Utopia,* claims both its value and its identity from its belief that it surpasses previous works of similar motivation because it is aligned with reality and not with mere verbal exercise. In the main body of the work, the claim to reality is acted out in the formalism of both books, where first the conversation with Hythloday and then his "report" of his travels are offered as historical events. Moreover, the subject of the opening conversation seriously considers the actual possibility of shaping real events through intellectual counsel. When these facts of the work are joined with the real facts of new discovery, of printing, of new culture, one sees that the overriding moment of the work's social intention is the excitement of *real possibility*—the possibility not only of a transformation of human life, but much more importantly, the possibility for the world of words to, so to speak, "become flesh." The decisive change in the nature of intellectuality that More was wrestling with was that here might indeed be the instrument of "utopian" transformation. What pushed utopia into conceptual usage, therefore, was the covert recognition, symbolized by the pun, Eutopia, brewing throughout the age, that the world of words that framed classical wishes might now claim to bring these wishes about. Possibility defends the fantasy by justifying it.

Yet it remains true that it was the word "utopia," and not "eutopia," that entered and remained in the language, much as *Utopia* was kept as the title of the work in spite of the ruminations of the kingdom's poet laureate. The retention of this term as the work's title, moreover, is of a piece with the apology at the conclusion of the work.

> I readily admit that there are very many features in the Utopian commonwealth which it is easier for me to wish for in our countries than to have any hope of seeing realized.[2]

Both statements, title and conclusion, express the paradox of possibility: the indeterminateness intrinsic to the recognition of the wish's plausibility, along with the capacity to—more than express it—communicate it, garners assent of its closeness to reality, *but does not actually fulfill this wish.* The denotative meaning of the word, "nowhere," expresses its own remoteness from reality and even, in a sense, asserts its own unreality. Yet, this assertion is compensatory in the sense that it urges the confounding of itself with its pun, which expresses, all too immodestly, the work's motivating impulse to victory and reality. In their excitement with the possibility, both ends of the pun oppose each other with the extremes of response, which, ironically, manage to subvert the rationality of possibility. It seems that the freshness and the surprise of possibility threaten an apparent comfort implicit in the condition of pure wishfulness so that the intensity of such wishfulness is redoubled even as the objective need for it is lessened. The important fact about this dynamic is not only that it operates the word utopia, which seems to be the only survivor of all efforts to extend its cultural range, but that it also operates pretwentieth-century intellectuality itself in an age—the post-Renaissance age—of ever enlarging material possibility. Insofar as intellectuality has been at the frontier of most attempts at complex formal elaboration of utopia, it becomes clear that this mode of social adaptation has exacerbated the excesses of the wish it is trying to reconcile. After the decline of utopia at the end of the Transition, intellectuality takes over the role sought by the utopian, and thus shorn of the uncompromising wish, tries to cope with the uncertainties of possibility. It is not until the twentieth century that intellectuality through the emergence of the professional expert, was able to make a widespread bid for meaningful social participation.

Thinking back for a moment to the pre-More millenarian period in Europe, early forms of modern intellectuality seem to correspond with the early forms of the utopian fantasy. The millenarian prophet, writes Cohn, "was not a manual worker . . . but an intellectual or half-intellectual."[3] The leader, that is, was usually a disaffected monk or priest, one who knew at least—but usually considerably more than—snippets of sources, but who was able to combine his knowledge with his charisma. Aside from the primary fantasy material operating here, there is a realistic, even adult perception of the impotence of words, a recognition that words alone will not do for a lifetime. The attempt is made, however primitive, anarchic, and futile, to accord referential meaning to the words people have been repeating since childhood. Whatever the unconscious motivation, in short, language was now being asked not merely for an installment, but full payment, at last, on its long-promised note of hope. As we know, for many centuries no widespread progress was made to secure systematic, institutional rights for intellectual endeavor because it was too expensive given all the other entrenched interests. But when the age of big science, technology, and industry came in full strength during the Transition, the need and the room for intellectual work became considerably more than marginal, much as the probability of at least local success became realistic.

In the meantime, many critics have observed, the utopian mind became an amalgam of infantile fantasy and intellectual idealism. The result was odd at best. Raymond Ruyer writes, for example, that

La combinason de l'esprit spéculatif et de l'esprit de puissance chez l'utopiste est d'un genre très particulier. Il s'agit chez lui d'un *rêve* de pouvoir, et d'une compensation adlerienne pour l'impuissance congenitale de la theorie pure. Il s'agit d'une 'projection' de la theorie dans une sphère étrangère.[4]

Given the circumstances of increasing technological possibility, the old intellectual dream of power acquired a new but very nervous urgency. But even as reality encouraged the religious hope growing from the infantile fantasy, it underscored the "impotence" congenital to pure speculation, so that possibility itself seemed an illusion, and the need for real outlet became ever more insistent. In more modern terms, utopianism might be said to have been caught in a neurotic paralysis, which, as in the individual, inhibits full-scale functioning, though never really halts the machinery. J.T. Flynn writes, accordingly, that "utopias always fail" in their final aim because utopianism "is an occupational disease of intellectualism."[5] For a long time, to have been an intellectual was to run the constant risk of inner frustration and social scorn because of the enforced discrepancy between symbolic power and actual power.

The critical tack taken by students of utopianism after the historical experience of the Nazi millenium is certainly a response to the latent ruthlessness of the intellectual posture of utopianism. Bertrand Russell views Plato "with as little reverence as if he were a contemporary English or American advocate of totalitarianism."[6] Behind the grandiose idealist, Russell sees "a well-to-do aristocrat, related to various people who were concerned in the rule of the Thirty Tyrants,"[7] and whose youthful observation of the defeat of Athens by Sparta conditioned his subsequent sympathy for the Spartan elitism and discipline. In addition, Negley and Patrick note that Lycurgus's plan for Sparta "proved to be an early Fascist state"[8] complete with cultic militarism and infanticide. Lurking behind what Negley and Patrick name as the "stock ideas of utopists . . . equality of the sexes, natural religion; the brotherhood of man, toleration . . . dedication to virtue or to justice,"[9] and several others—Karl Popper finds a "neurotic and even hysterical element . . . the ethics of hero-worship . . . which can understand life only in terms of 'dominate or submit.' "[10] Rita Falke states baldly that "the theoreticians and politicians of totalitarian states recognize the components of ancient utopias as similar and suitable to their own practice."[11] Plato's state itself, she notes, is built "in his own words" on "a single thoroughly well-intentioned lie."[12] The utopian story, she winds up,

ends with the destruction of the individual . . . when there is no longer any individual action, we have the virtual end of history. And that, since time immemorial, is the aim of every utopia.[13]

While it is true that the academic "discovery" of a motivating totalitarianism in utopian thinking is partially conditioned by a spontaneous concern with the recent German social disaster, it is equally clear that the autocratic impulse was long implicit in any kind of idealism and particularly in utopian visions. Nazism simply found the social technology—and the uniquely aberrant leader—to utilize the elements of an almost universal popular utopian impulse and to proclaim in a loud voice and frenzied jubilance what most dared not admit in normal conversation and disinterested scrutiny: "Somewhere deep inside me, I want the world for myself; in fact, I want us to be identical: *'Ein Volk, Ein Reich, Ein Furhrer.'* " Psychic energy and technological possibility combined in the power of the ultimate Big Brother.

Hence, Ruyer's indication of the *"compensation adlerienne."*

> Beaucoup d'utopistes mineurs sont des faibles qui protestent contre la realité parce qu'ils n'y peuvent jouer un rôle à leur convenance, et qui cherchant une compensation à leur faiblesse.
> Dans leur monde imaginaire, ils peuvent donner la toute-pusissance au type d'homme qu'ils representent.[14]

Students of utopianism likewise began noticing that the utopian drama is a thinly disguised social projection of the personal wishes of the utopist, in a mode more clearly discernable than the modes of any other kind of social or professional enterprise. The utopian situation calls for the continual directives of some Ur-leader, some King Utopus to "found" the society, who, by virtue of his ability to imagine the situation to begin with, must be some kind of intellectual, and thus on a more respectably exalted plateau than the masses of illiterate poor. Much as Antonio tells Gonzalo that "yet thou would be king on"[15] his imaginary commonwealth, Marie Berneri notes that "the majority of the builders of utopias are determined to remain the masters in their imaginary communities."[16] As Erikson has already noted, the importance of *Mein Kampf* was that it created a national legend of the life of the leader, a new kind of bible, a source that at once depersonalized and dignified the unconscious popular need to play out the stories themselves. In the utopian complex of values, the book—the word, the speech, the law—in short, all the major intellectual institutions of civilization are fused with the "flesh" of the utopist. This grotesque longing, much as it duplicates the primary utopian fantasy of union with mother and identity with the world, has long been inherent in the allegedly remote area of intellectual scholarly endeavor, and has remained an implicit compensatory wish of those men—as opposed to women—undertaking such apparently austere and rational commitments.

Andrew Hacker, suggesting that utopias are "usually written by mild and scholarly people,"[17] is himself one of a group of "mild and scholarly" critics who are not deeply alarmed by the totalism of intellectuality. In part, the outward calm of these critics comes from a stance of secure objectivity. But the range and texture of their studies, along with a revealing critical habit, suggests that their acceptance of utopianism on the basis of its mildness is motivated by feelings similar to those of the utopists themselves. In a strange but significant sense these critics are submitting to utopian "rules." Most of their studies are surveys of utopianism from the beginning to the end, or to the present. Each work or phase of utopia is duly reviewed, and a brief comment is offered so that one gets an overall picture. There is something unusually unscholarly about these "mild and scholarly" studies.[18] Specifically, these studies explicitly overtake the utopian metaphor of the journey and geographical discovery so that the typically utopian posture informs the presumably more objective critical posture. Oscar Wilde writes that "a map of the world that does not include Utopia is not even worth glancing at." It is the "one country at which Humanity is always landing."[19] Frances Russell begins *Touring Utopia* aiming to "bring back heightened perceptions of the values of our home planets freshened appreciations of their brighter future and greater possibilities."[20] Lewis Mumford invites, "our ship is about to sail; and we shall not heave anchor again until we reach the coasts of Utopia."[21] And Negley and Patrick, whose study is more reliable and balanced than most, indicate that "the land of utopia has never been properly or completely charted." They remark at the "rather famous landmarks along the flat plains of the shore," at the "familiar sights to the traveller on literary excursions," at the "shifting currents," at the "shore of utopia," the "salubrious climate" in the "mysterious land of light and shadow" whose "natives are, almost to a man, very friendly and generous."[22] In all of these happy metaphors, as in the larger structure of the works they introduce, there is a peculiar sentimentality, a boyish, adolescent excitement, and even the self-same utopian wish for a happy land, at once mysterious and reassuring, with benign, generous "natives." Much as the intellectual features of utopianism are compromised by this adolescent mood, so many critical studies in the early modern period sacrifice their critical adulthood to the pageantry of the utopian fantasy.

In the English-speaking world, therefore, intellectual appraisal of utopianism and its importance to civilization has been significantly slow to recognize its inherent bankruptcy—or at least its essential irrelevance in modern times. While Negley and Patrick admit that utopias were simply not written after about 1910, they remark that "it is to the utopists of the future that we shall look for the design and detail of the new ideal."[23] Likewise, Kenneth Keniston traces the "decline of utopia" to the "cultural change . . . from commitment and enthusiasm to alienation and apathy,"[24] and claims that to regain "positive morality" men must "now resolve their alienations by committing themselves to the preparation for new utopias."[25] Even as it is observed that utopias are no longer a tangible part of modern intellectual effort, the sense of their necessity remains in the wish that they will reappear in the future and in the belief that they are somehow necessary to the ethical welfare of human beings.

The regressive quality and psychological recalcitrance of the wish appear most clearly as they infiltrate the work of two contemporary social scientists who cannot be viewed in the older categories of utopianism: Paul Goodman and B.F. Skinner. At some point in their work, which for the most part is concerned with problems fairly well circumscribed in social or psychological reality, the emotional expectations of reality are so great that they overwhelm a potentially aggressive but realistic sense of possibility. Goodman observes with justification that "a hint of change" in our society "disturbs our resignation and rouses our anxiety."[26] Anticipating resistance to his social proposals, he characterizes them as "common sense and direct action toward obvious good."[27] On reading his proposal to ban all cars from Manhattan Island, however, it is plain that here is not merely a "hint of change" nor "obvious good." In fact, from the point of view of the million or so residents of Manhattan, the suggestion seeks a total transformation of life in Manhattan coupled with a covert wish to make trouble for the many whose life-habits depend on their automobiles. The utopian stamp of his thinking emerges from the juxtaposition of a rational, commonsense self-conception with the irrational, subtly violent wish for total social overhaul. In defining his own "psychology as a Utopian sociologist," Goodman makes this thought pattern explicit, as he writes in what must be taken as a truly deviant but here revealing mood,

> I am concerned not for material improvement or safety, but for conservation or innovation in our culture and humane ideals. I feel myself and my colleagues to be in special touch with the holy spirit.[28]

Much as the "holy spirit" of the religious election motivated the millenarian prophet, it here appears, behind the guise of contemporary rationality, to create a neo-utopian anachronism, repeating, in vestigial form, the classic utopian fantasy through which the inner infant is projected onto and merged with external reality.

The situation is analogous with Skinner, who, having worked a lifetime in the laboratory perfecting ways of controlling and predicting animal behavior, created a fantasy, *Walden Two,* in which the narrator imagines himself writing an obscene telegram to the university president, telling him (in capital letters) to "take your stupid university . . ."[29] while he goes off to join a utopian colony run on the principles of "behavioral engineering." The architect of this community, pretty clearly an effigy of both the author's and the narrator's alter ego, had long ago abjured the academy for this new experiment, and by the end of the novel appears in his naked fantasy form. On the top of a ledge called the "Throne," the narrator observes:

> He was lying flat on his back, his arms stretched out at full length. His legs were straight but his ankles were lightly crossed. He allowed his head to fall limply to one side, and I reflected that his beard made him look a little like Christ. Then, with a shock, I saw that he had assumed the position of the crucifixion.[30]

The hero, Frazier, also like the millenarian prophet, is an intellectual manqué, who, unlike Skinner himself, committed his life to a new quest for realization instead of remaining in the academic pale. Skinner has indicated that he remains in the academic world because he knows how good it is and how risky the "utopian" experiment would be.[31] Yet the informing emotion of his scientific zeal has always strained beyond the animal laboratory, even beyond the aim of understanding human behavior, but finally and decisively to *control* it. In a subsequently published interview, he, like Goodman, seems to recognize the religious motive operating within him without really grasping its full import. "I may feel guilty about my Puritan heritage," he tells the interviewer; he then rhetorically wonders about "world improvement": "Is it up to me?"[32] Ever since More, when the millenarian fantasy first acquired its social pretext of "improvement" through an intellectual machinery, this otherwise valuable machinery, when attached to the utopian wish—the "up to me" fantasy—has not only itself been compromised, but also has itself fostered the disappearance of utopianism as a cultural force.

This disappearance is played out in the larger historical transformation to a state of somewhat less grandiose but more realistic view of social progress. Relatively early in the century, though more or less obscurely, the change was viewed as part of the natural process of intellectual development. In one of the first historical studies of utopianism, Joyce Hertzler writes that

> with the perfecting of theories of history and the growth of the idea of development, real utopias ceased to appear, for men now had a conception of social growth and development, and were not confronted with the necessity of picturing a perfect substitute for, but of making improvement in present society.[33]

This, in part, is true, but it does not really account for the abruptness of the change. Utopianism began with a relatively discrete series of historical events all within very few years of each other. The onset of the twentieth century witnessed a series of likewise discrete technological events that, in effect, reversed the emotional precipitates of the beginning of utopianism: those "utopian" wishes that had been heretofore only possibilities were now either actualities or imminent actualities. As George Woodcock has observed:

> Though so much of the utopian dream is being fulfilled, planned societies have brought little marked increase in human happiness.[34]

He concludes that "the error seems to be in the utopian outlook itself."[35] The public forms of the utopian fantasy, since they were rooted in the intellectual perception of possibility, were *crippled by the fulfillment of the possibility*. The arrival of large-scale technology essentially separated the generating fantasy from its intellectual justifications, so that within the last five or six decades both fantasy and justifications have developed identities of their own with the resulting disappearance of the traditional utopia.

Technology and mass literacy imbued intellectual work with a new utility so that it no longer depended altogether on its alliance with infantile wishes. Utopianism has been replaced, Daniel Bell wrote, by "the study of the future,"[36] and he names more than ten full-length studies of what might really happen in the future—not only in the next few years, but also in the next decades and even the next centuries. "The apocalyptic modes of thought that dominated the 19th century," that were "nourished by utopian vision of earthly abundance, and the irrationalist pessimism derived from aristocratic, Catholic, and Nietzschean critiques of mass society," and which "culminated in the Soviet effort to transform a lumbering society root and branch" and in "the Nazi glorification of race and blood," have "largely disappeared among the Western intelligentsia."[37] The technology that fulfilled the material possibility also exposed the madness of fulfilling the infantile emotional possibility, an exposure resulting in the exhaustion of the utopian vision. The remains of this crisis in utopianism have initiated a new attitude toward its original rationality.

> What has remained from the utopian tradition, however, and this is the underlying element in our renewed interest in the future, is its eudaemonism—the proposition that each person is entitled to happiness and that it is one of the functions of government to try and assure him at least the preconditions of happiness.[38]

When Herbert Marcuse suggested that the burgeoning computer technology implied "a new basic experience of being [that] would change human existence in its entirety,"[39] it was realized that this claim was more realistic than utopian. Subsequently, students of computerization and its possibilities, notably Alice Hilton, have observed that "cybernation . . . *eliminates any need* for human labor [toil as opposed to work]" and that "within a decade or two we can have full abundance and leisure."[40] In the place of incomplete visions of complete social transformation, we now find organized confrontation of social possibility by less-than-visionary professionals. Divested of its apocalyptic imperative, utopia is the domain of "real" intellectuals—psychologists, sociologists, political scientists, economists—while the word "utopia" rests with analogous reality in our vocabularies, denoting a phrase in the development of civilization, a state of mind no longer helpful.

It makes sense, then, as Negley and Patrick observe, that "contemporary utopian fantasies are more likely to reflect literary skill than profound social or political significance."[41] Utopias, in other words, are now consciously created as fantasies, as opposed to their having originally operated as fantasies under the illusion of their realizability. The removal of the utopian fantasy into the *content* of fantasy and "literary skill" permitted a free expression and manipulation of the actual fantasy content—the naked violence of the dynamics of rebellion and domination. As "utopia has moved from nowhere to now-here," George Knox observes, "as the gap between fiction and reality closed, with alarming speed, dark eschatologies took over the imaginations of the fantasists.''[42] What makes these ''eschatologies'' especially dark is their exposure of the hitherto latent component of the oedipal fantasy, the component only implicit in the ''eutopia's'' feeling of victory over his rival—the intense fear that the rival may win over it. Thus, the two most important of the modern fantasies, *Brave New World* and *1984,* dwell on the ruthless subjugation of the familiar half-intellectual hero. The adolescent hero, in each case trying to define his identity against impossible odds, is not merely defeated but locked in the original infantile state of total helplessness. The issue is drawn in the same terms of utopian totality, but instead of the total identification with Big Brother there is total estrangement. The intellectual idealism of utopia having taken a practical turn, the continuing infantile fear not only of helplessness, but of punishment for attempting to overrule the prevailing authority, emerges in all its extremism.

Whether or not, as Adam Ulam has suggested, ''we have reached a moratorium if not indeed the end of utopias,''[43] the transformation of traditional utopianism at the outset of the twentieth century is commensurate in both scope and significance with the transformation it had undergone when the word first entered our vocabularies at the outset of the sixteenth century. Where, in More's age, we might say that the millenarian fantasy and the intellectual life were married, giving birth to a large family of immature children, in the Transition the marriage ended, and each partner realized, in a sense, its need for a more fulfilling context of operation. The fantasy, deprived of its old religious contexts, yet remaining basic to human beings, entered more unambiguously into the world long related to the transcendental, the world of art, and there produced tangible contributions to this world. The intellectual idealism, meanwhile, also acquired a new context, the civilization of mass technology and mass literature. Yet before this division became clear as the twentieth century wore on, the Transition seems to have witnessed what must be utopia's finest hour, an unprecedented efflorescence and mass popularity, a profound social inquiry into utopianism, apparently gaining a new foothold in human culture. Yet this climax was a preamble to demise; the forces of the Transition that raised utopia to new importance were those whose ultimate emergence in the twentieth century precluded its continued existence.

# 4

# Transition Fantasy and Victorian Childhood

Utopia in the Transition years attained its most formidable proportions. Historians in general agree that, as Louis Budd suggests, "by 1890 . . . western man seemed to be working busily toward general happiness."[1] On one hand, the power of technology to create mass quantities of consumer goods and to reproduce its own wealth gave the public a taste of utopian abundance and persuaded it of its imminence; on the other hand, the enfranchisement of science and intellectual work, its increasing accessibility to greater numbers of people, offered a tangible institutional space, a viable social structure through which this abundance might be both regulated and maintained. Even science, through Darwin's documentation that the "fittest" survive, suggested that it was in the nature of phylogenetic functioning that a utopian state of mankind was not merely desirable but inevitable. Karl Marx, also, even in his denial of the "utopian" meaning of socialism, had asserted that history itself will bring about the ancient wish for an egalitarian condition of humanity. "Why not now," it could easily be imagined, "why not, with such new empirical understanding of the social processes, with such powerful new material capacities; utopia must surely be but a step away." For this reason, John Flanagan says, of the end of the nineteenth century, that "probably never before and never since has it [the idea of Progress] been accepted with such complete conviction."[2] This might well have been Oscar Wilde's point when he wrote that "progress is the realisation of utopias."[3] The great boost in the value of utopian stock, in other words, the new faith in the realizability of utopia, is an extra bonus created by the emergence in the Transition period of the traditional utopian intellectual justification, which we might now identify as the idea of Progress toward the apparently limitless possibilities of scientific understanding and technological power.

The idea of Progress, as an ideological defense of utopianism in the Transition, plays a role analogous to that played by Christian Humanism with respect to the first utopian age of More. Specifically, both movements were emotionally driven by a religious fantasy; they were different historical forms of old religious impulses. Ernest Tuveson's *Millenium and Utopia,* which could be seen as a historical sequel to Cohn's *Pursuit of the Millenium,* documents the constant conjunction, in the interval between the sixteenth and nineteenth centuries, of the idea of Progress and the apocalyptic wish. It is fairly common knowledge, for example, that from Boyle, through Newton, through eighteenth-century rationalism, the scientific discovery of order in the universe gained acceptance by presupposing that this order was manifestation of a divine teleology. Less known, however, is Edward Young's observation in 1759, quoted by Tuveson as the best summary of the thematic identity of divine and natural order:

> *since,* this world is a school, as well for intellectual, as moral, advance; and the longer human nature is at school, the better scholar it should be; *since,* as the moral world expects its glorious millennium, the world intellectual may hope, by the rules of analogy for some superior degrees of excellence to crown her later scenes.[4]

As a result, Tuveson concludes, that

> it was the Apocalypse, which at the beginning of the Reformation seemed only to augur a dark future for humanity, became, with the assistance of a new scientific philosophy of universal law, and encouraged by the great advances of knowledge of nature, the very guarantee and assurance of progress. . . . At the time of Bacon, the question was one of *possibility* of progress; within a hundred years, possibility became a certainty in men's faith.[5]

The years between More and the Transition witnessed, through the idea of Progress, the development of an interim world view that projected onto religion the feeling of certainty—namely the millenarian impulses—while retaining in reality the compromise view of progress. In any given utopia the two views— the affective certainty recognizable as the fantasy, progress as its rationalized form—coalesced, thus performing the ''siphoning off'' function while allowing the bifurcation to remain in the culture at large. The growth of technology some decades before the Transition allowed the ''siphon'' situation and the real situation to resemble each other more and more, until at the height of the period they were essentially indistinguishable: the writers and the planners comingled with each other. We thus encounter the strange situation in the Transition where an unprecedented rational assault on the problems of eudaemonism is driven at crucial points by a resurgence of the much older eschatological fantasies, so that utopianism, as George Knox observes,

> was a well-established mystique by the end of the nineteenth century: an extension of the Christian gospel on one hand and social-political organicism on the other.[6]

Both in England and America, the gospelizing of social reform movements struck an important keynote of popular consciousness. In England W.H.G. Armytage reports that Henry George's *"Progress and Poverty* (1879) was received . . . (as William Morris said) 'as a new gospel.' "[7] Significantly, this reception is not a purely subjective function of the socio-religious preoccupations of Morris and his like; it is traceable, rather, to the work itself, whose intellectual burden leads to a conclusion revealing its emotional undertow. "What then is the meaning of life—of life absolutely and inevitably bounded by death?" George asks at the end of his treatise.

To me it seems intelligible only as the avenue and vestibule to another life.

Lo! here, now in our civilized society, the old allegories [Eden, etc.] yet have a meaning, the old myths are still true. Into the Valley of the Shadow of Death yet often leads the path of duty, through the streets of Vanity Fair walk Christian and Faithful, and on Greatheart's armor ring the clanging blows. Ormuzd still fights with Ahriman—the Prince of Light with the Powers of Darkness. He who will hear, to him the clarions of battle call.

How they call, and call, and call, till the heart swells that hears them! Strong soul and high endeavor, the world needs them now. Beauty still lies imprisoned, and iron wheels go over the good and true and beautiful that might spring from human lives.

The hope that rises in the heart of all religions! [as Plutarch said]:

"Men's souls, . . . when they are loosed from the body, and removed into the unseen, invisible, impassable, and pure region, this God is then their leader and king; they there, as it were, hanging on him wholly, and beholding without weariness and passionately affecting that beauty which cannot be expressed or uttered by men."[8]

Neither George nor those of his persuasion actually proposed to fuse disembodied souls with God in the pure unseen region. But the sheer presence of the *fantasy* of such fusion bespeaks the presence, in the ostensibly intellectual proposal of the "single tax," of the familiar wish for social fusion, even a total amalgamation of all culture, following heroically upon the final call to battle. The single tax is implicitly a universal tax, a machinery for homogenizing the human race according to its most characteristically infantile wishes.

George's near hysterical reception in England, furthermore, found significant sympathetic analogues. The Labor Movement, founded as it was by the Fabians and other practical people, seemed nevertheless to attract this same kind of emotional excess. Armytage reports that in 1892 John Trevor founded the Labor Church "for the distinct purpose of declaring that God is at work, here and now, in the heart of the Labour Movement."[9] The movement itself, of course, did not need this reassurance as much as Trevor himself did, who thus sought out God in his social domain of the "meek" proletariat. The case is similar for Noel Buxton, Armytage indicates, quoting Mosa Anderson's biography. Buxton left the liberals and joined the Labor Church because

the Kingdom of God is still a collective conception involving the whole social life of man. . . .
It is not a matter of getting individuals to heaven, but of transforming the life on earth into the
harmony of heaven.[10]

On the level of emotional fantasy, what difference can there be between getting
people to heaven and getting heaven to people? The merger is in any case the
desired end. At the periphery of the Labor Movement, then, much as at the
periphery of the more or less realistic Peasant Revolt, there appears the familiar
impulse toward immediate heaven, a god that is working "here and now" at the
task of establishing heaven on earth. The utopians inhabited this periphery and
both their personalities and their works partook in large drafts of such Labor
Church thinking, except that it was they who viewed themselves as the instruments of heavenly salvation, who were working for utopia "here and now."
Morris must have been grateful to find a "gospel" to clear the way for his New
Jerusalem.

Because in America, as Allyn Forbes claims,[11] there was no discernable
influence of utopianism and Christian Socialism, it is all the more striking
that almost identical kinds of movements arose at essentially the same times.
This fact suggests that the popular utopian fantasy is more likely to be a co-
feature of major technological change than the result of trans-Atlantic resonance
or intellectual sympathy. The "social gospel" in America functioned in a mode
analogous to, but far more intense than, the Labor Church in England. Timothy
Smith states that the "ideology of the millenium merged without a break into
what came to be called the social gospel." This gospel began proclaiming in the
midnineteenth century that *"all* is *Progress,"* and that, as Smith portrays it,

Christianity and culture seemed to be marching together, "onward and upward" toward the
"grand consummation of prophecy in a civilized, and enlightened, and a sanctified world" and
the establishment of "that spiritual kingdom which God has ordained shall triumph and en-
dure."[12]

The lectures of the social gospelers

were heard by the thousands, its books read by hundreds of thousands, and incalculable numbers joined its organizations or attended its earnest conferences.[13]

Richard Hofstadter suggests that because of this, one of its important "accom-
plishments was to break ground for the Progressive era."[14] This is probably
most vividly characterized by Bryan's almost evangelical campaign for the
Presidency; his threat of "crucifixion" for America coincided with the peak of
utopian popularity. In the decade of the nineties, Forbes counts[15] the publication
of at least 50 utopian novels, which R.L. Shurter indicates "were read by the
millions, many of whom regarded them as the hope of civilization."[16] Out of
the Populist and utopian strains in American society, observes Clinton Keeler,

the "symbols of the popular imagination" joined together in a quest for a "deeply desired unity."[17] "The Reformers felt," Keeler continues,

> that popular government, the basis of all their proposals, must depend upon a community of belief. One set of beliefs centered in the mythology of primitivism, but another centered in the mythology of utopian progress. The intensity of the search for unity is reflected in the religious symbolism—the "religion of humanity." In the gulf separating the dream of anarchic primitivism from the dream of utopian progress we see the American folk pursuing their unending quest for brotherhood.[18]

While the linkage of primitivism and progress is familiar enough as the common utopian formula, the ideal of brotherhood has a special American ring to it. The idea itself is of course not peculiarly American, but America is the same new world that was discovered when utopia first entered the cultural scene. The founding of the country, as D.H. Lawrence suggested some time ago, was attended less by an idealism than by a "black revulsion from Europe," the impulse to be free "even [of] God Almighty."[19] The resultant brotherhood and democracy were at least as much motivated by the anarchic will to destroy the "old authority of Europe"[20] and to proclaim no masters at all. There is a determining element of vengeance in the ideal of brotherhood that reminds us of the emotional excesses of the millenarian prophets, themselves "brothers" of the ever present "Free Spirit." In a sense, utopianism was part of the American national character from the founding of the country.

American national psychology during the Transition thus offers an especially compelling paradigm for how the utopian fantasy operated in general. In particular, American psychology was adolescent from the outset, precipitated by the Puritan crisis of religious identity, and afterward enshrined in the oldest successful revolution in the western world. The subsequent continuing state of pluralism in the country, perpetuated at every point by new immigrants from new countries, as well as new frontiers and new boundaries, made for a continuing struggle for identity, a continuing psychology of adolescence. During the technological boom of the late nineteenth century, this struggle reached its near hysterical pitch and made for heroes such as Dreiser's Financier, the unscrupulous, sexually unstable millionaire searching for ever greater power and ever younger women. If, as Russell Nye has characterized it, the American Transition is one from "nineteenth century adolescence to twentieth century maturity,"[21] it is a period that in a crucial sense recapitulates in especially intense form a determining growth pattern of American civilization, the perpetual struggle for a mature national identity. This intensification on the larger scale seems to underlie the unusual gush of utopian sentiment during this period.

In America, the violence implicit in the utopian fantasy and its adolescent machinery found its expression, in sublimated form, in the real world, mainly in the new territory of the West, where each man (as opposed to each woman) was notoriously his own law, though also in the East, where the Robber Barons were likewise exempted from legal constraint. In England, however, there was no frontier, and economic violence was internally limited by the deep historical roots of the class structure, yet it appeared externally in empire building. Nevertheless, the expected violence was unmistakably present and clearly related, if not also dependent on the great wave of utopian enthusiasm. Where in America the murder and theft was consciously justified as a sacrifice to the creation of wealth, the violent fantasies in England seemed to appear as if an expression of guilt for the similarly unscrupulous process of empire building. The same Oscar Wilde who wrote that "progress is the fulfillment of Utopias" suggested that the condition of *fin de siècle* was governed by a feeling of *fin du globe*.[22] This reactive fear, Bernard Bergonzi indicates, was expressed in a striking series of *fin du globe* novels, whose tales recall vividly, but in reverse, the visions of the medieval chiliasts. The usual scheme was a fantasy of the invasion of England by some inscrutable alien force—either Chinese or the plague—in which utter devastation was the inevitable outcome. "These novels," Bergonzi observes,

> with their images of physical destruction, showing the fair face of England desecrated by foreign troops, afford an obvious parallel to the moral and intellectual shock administered to bourgeois complacency and self-confidence by Ibsen and the aesthetes. Indeed, it is hard to resist the conclusion that a certain collective death-wish pervaded the national consciousness at the time, despite its superficial assertiveness and brash jingoism.[23]

Psychoanalytically speaking, the assertiveness and jingoism informing British imperialism must have occasioned such fantasied fears of retribution at the hands of the subjugated races. The form of these fantasies represents only a slight variation of the usual form of the utopian fantasy. This binds the utopian, the imperialistic, and the fear-of-retribution emotions into the familiar syndrome of the utopian fantasy: a thrust, both actual and imagined, for possession of the world occasions a release of nervous energy, both excessively fearsome and excessively hopeful, that represents the breakthrough of infantile traumas into the social identity now being threatened by the changing century. *Fin de siècle,* Bergonzi thus notes, represents a primary emotional substrate of this period, a characteristic ambivalence attending a change of identity.

> In England this mood was heightened by the feeling that Queen Victoria's reign had also lasted excessively long. But at the same time, no one knew what the coming twentieth century was going to bring, though there was no lack of speculation. The result could be described as a certain loss of nerve, weariness with the past, combined with foreboding about the future. The *fin de siècle* mood produced . . . the feeling of *fin du globe,* the sense that the whole elaborate intellectual and social order of the nineteenth century was trembling on the brink of dissolution.[24]

The term *"fin"* in both of these catchphrases suggests that at the deepest level, the anxiety was less about the onset of the new century than about the necessity to renounce the old, much as it was in More's age, where the old church was so much more entrenched in society than Victorianism was now. The Victorian outlook, in any case, held especially powerful roots in its constituents and offers psychological documentation for British utopianism analogous to that offered by American national adolescence to American utopianism. The common image of Victoria as a repressed and repressive mother figure can be taken, psychologically, at face value. Walter Houghton's study of Victorian culture suggests that the customary adult thought style is marked by the tendency to exaggerate masculine heroism and feminine delicacy, leading to the image of parents as nonsexual figures.[25] Queen Victoria is a national symbol of this means of collective self-management. Mothers become as in "the Prince's description of his mother in [Tennyson's] *The Princess,*"

> No angel, but a dearer being, all dipt,
> In angel instincts, breathing Paradise,
> Interpreter between the gods and men . . .[26]

But father is the embodiment of the values worshipping physical force and military heroes; fathers were supposed to be like medieval knights, bearing almost magical strength and goodness. As Houghton suggests, the heroic image of the parents and the general value of hero-worship are related to the sense of heroes and leaders as messianic.[27] Salvation, and not only amelioration, is the feeling behind the characteristic Victorian earnestness, purity, and diligence. Houghton shows how, in mid-nineteenth century, these values of messianic salvation and hero-worship became part of the utopian hopes which grew from technological achievements and Darwinian thinking that implied the privileged character of human beings. While adolescents themselves were not heroic figures in Victorian times, one can see that values we now think of as adolescent were actually appearing in adult mentalities. These values were passed on to the "utopian" generation.

Whatever the antecedent causes, the latter half of the nineteenth century shows, in both England and America, the rapidly rising prominence of an adolescent world outlook that motivated the sudden efflorescence of the utopian vision. The snowballing necessity to renounce this adolescent outlook precipitated its massive projection into the utopian world; it fostered, that is, the joining of the real world with the utopian world, the mixing of real impulses and peripheral ones in a flurry of tremendous excitement—but also of tremendous ambivalence. The classical utopian values were learned by the utopists as values of their own childhood—the "Victorian" values of both England and America —and then, as the threat of rapid social change became a certainty, these values of childhood were marshalled with redoubled enthusiasm in a hysterical effort to save them from being undermined. Because all adults living in the Transition must, of necessity, have had Victorian childhoods, the general population was threatened with the identical fate as were the utopists. The threat being as widespread as it was, massive sales of utopian novels resulted, along with the communities, the political organizations, the religious sects, and, of course, the end-of-the-world literature. The Victorian ethic—the characteristic system of Victorian cultural self-management—reached its climax in the extremism of utopian benevolence, underneath which there pressed for realization the old religious wish-fantasy for the restoration of infantile totality whose temporary Victorian equilibrium was now "on the brink of dissolution."

Two childhoods of prominent Victorians (the childhoods of two of the three most prominent utopians) offer a persuasive paradigm of how this psychological configuration actually worked and how it led to the subsequent turn to manifest utopianism. Although the topical personalities of Edward Bellamy and William Morris are usually taken to represent opposed views—even diametrically opposed views—of utopianism, significant trends in their respective childhoods suggest not only that they were motivated by similar types of fantasies, but also that their visible forms of self-management (the adult utopian identities of the two men), which seem to be so different, are likewise similarly defined by struggles with the same problem. These struggles, furthermore, suggest how the utopian fantasy ultimately reached its more permanent twentieth-century context in the world of art, how the fantasy itself made its own transition and thereby acted out the much larger cultural transition undergone by the two nations.

In Morris's review of Bellamy's *Looking Backward*. J.W. Mackail finds the "single sentence [that] contains the sum of his [Morris's] belief in politics, in economics, in art."[28]

> Mr. Bellamy worries himself unnecessarily in seeking, with obvious failure, some incentive to labour to replace the fear of starvation which is at present our only one; whereas it cannot be too often repeated that the true incentive to useful and happy labour is, and must be, pleasure in the work itself.[29]

There is, of course, especially in terms of psychologically informed values, no arguing with this principle: love of one's work is a necessity for psychosocial wellbeing, and many cite this idea of Morris's as truly advanced. Yet the essential import of the idea as well as its psychological underpinnings is defined more fully by the context that created it than the value we now accord it. Mackail informs us that the idea, though part of Morris's life outlook from the beginning, was spurred to its full expression in *News from Nowhere* as a direct reaction to the "apotheosis of machinery and the glorification of the life of large towns in"[30] *Looking Backward*. Thus a determining element of Morris's great commitment to enjoyable work is an implicit rejection of technology's imperative to view society on a mass scale. If, however, this rejection actually led to a fulfilling vocational commitment and to the kind of happiness so urgently envisioned in Nowhere, it should not arouse a pejorative judgment of such a rejection. As Philip Henderson observes, the unfortunate fact remains that Morris was "deeply frustrated in his personal life" and was "tormented by the thought that he had no right to immerse himself in this harmony while the greater part of the population of the country were condemned"[31] to social misery. "It may be," he concludes, "that this outraged social conscience had its roots in some deepseated guilt-feeling, but whatever its cause, Morris forsook his earlier position of art-for-art's sake and forced himself into politics."[32] We are thus led to the view that Morris's rejection of Bellamy's wide perspective is symptomatic of an inner tension between this perspective and his more personal —and more satisfying—impulses to pleasure.

It is no secret that, whatever his socialist views, Morris ultimately became an entrepreneur like his father, whose wealth played no small part in the development of his (Morris's) aesthetic longings, so that from the beginning a powerful individualist strain was developing. At least two of Morris's biographers have indicated that the life in Nowhere was less a romantic vision than "a very true account of Morris's own life among his own friends"[33] and that the old manor which the friends visit bears a remarkable resemblance to his own famous Kelmscott Manor. It is true, moreover, that at the beautiful Woodford Hall, where Morris spent his happiest childhood days, there was an unusual degree of self-sufficiency and insularity: "They kept their own horses, cows, pigs, chickens and rabbits, baked their own bread, made their own cheeses, and brewed their own beer,"[34] Eshleman reports. And yet another feature of this grand home is even more psychologically significant. Legend has it that Morris was a prodigy in reading and was able, at the age of four, to read Scott's Waverly novels. Whether he actually read them can remain moot, but that he was intimate with the stories is clear. So strongly did they capture his imagination, that for two years before moving to Woodford, he demanded from his parents a toy suit of armor and a pony, which were finally granted him at Woodford since there was now enough space. Holbrook Jackson tells how

> he roamed over Epping and Savernake pondering deeply upon the life of those beautiful places, giving them for himself and for those who then had his confidence, and for those who have since read his books, a new significance.[35]

A salient feature of his life, Jackson notes, however, was that it "was not a romance of actual deeds, but of colored dreams."[36] The implication is that even though the young Morris was surely only playing, this play held an uncommon seriousness for him, and to an abnormally large extent, it acted in the place of something patently missing from his real child's life. "He played his own game of life," Jackson continues, "and had his own intellectual method."[37] We also know that in his childhood, as well as in adulthood, he exhibited a violent temper, "and was thought a little mad by his schoolfellows," who still listened to his "endless stories about knights and fairies."[38] Finally, though relatively obscurely entered, Jackson notes: "It is recorded how his fingers must ever be handling something; and a story is told of how he gained relief from this restlessness by endless netting."[39]

These three important characteristics of his childhood—his imagination, his temper, and his manual activity—are all known aspects of his adult personality. Taken together, they seem to form a pattern. In particular, his imagination and his restlessness are of a piece with each other, for both are ultimately put into the service of art. Yet in childhood they seemed to behave as outlets for some other frustration, much as his quick temper testifies to his low tolerance of frustration. His handicrafts suggest the desire for an immediacy, a directness of outlet that certain inner needs apparently demanded. In later life he had to actually go to Iceland to collect the original material of the stories that captivated him. We might characterize a major aspect of his personality, therefore, by noting the tendency to close some gap between something buried in his imagination, probably unknown to him, and the material abundance surrounding him, to somehow identify these two resources, whose separation he neither understood nor resolved. But what are they, really, and how did Morris cope with them?

Between the two romances of childhood and Kelmscott, there intervened a less romantic and more painful adolescence and early youth. Although the consequences are not wholly clear, Morris's father died when Morris was 13, the onset of puberty. Before then his mother was also probably not readily accessible as she had six younger children, so that from puberty on, and probably before as well, William was forced to be a kind of loner and was away at school most of the time anyway. His unusually rich imaginative activity, including his many childhood poems and his public story-telling, played the role the parent might normally play in these beginnings of identity-formation. In imagining himself a great hero, the task of finding out who he thought he was was something he had to do by himself. Although he wrote to his mother at one point that "I do not hope to be great at all in anything,"[40] Mackail indicates that "civility to inferiors was certainly not one of his strong points" and that "the aristocratic temper of his youth would show itself even in his latest years."[41] It might be surmised that the necessity, after the death of his father, for finding his identity only from his peer situation, forced the continued repression of these aristocratic and heroic impulses, and this necessity must have begun at home in an attempt to transcend all his many siblings. The search for identity—for a vocation and place in life—during his days at Oxford tried to work out a compromise between these repressed impulses—these sources of excessive emotional energy—and the need for an accepting social milieu. The result of this compromise is the Morris we are already familiar with—the priest in the religions now permanently established in the vision of Nowhere. His utopia, like More's, was the imaginary adolescent fulfillment of his childhood wishes.

The letter to his mother precluding his own wish for greatness also announces his decision to give up taking holy orders and to commit his life to art and architecture. His choice of vocation represented to him a purchase of the deeply desired path to fulfillment and to the resolution of his inner conflict. Henderson suggests that since his childhood, "sensuality remained for him tainted with sin," and "the sensuousness of his nature expended itself on the textures of fabrics, fine wood, and stone."[42] His love of physical materials and nature is probably a substitute for the early scarcity of physical contact and love. In this aspect of his vocational choice, he may have compensated for the early sensual deprivation, the enforced renunciation of his actual mother (who hoped he would take orders), and he may also have chosen a more pliable, more controllable, object of his love. This substitution, obviously, could not have been fulfilling enough, not only because he remained a nervous person with "the most childlike simplicity,"[43] but also because the real need has to be met with the real thing—in this case, love. The necessity to retain the thought of religious commitment promoted by his mother, and to work that in somehow both out of respect and ultimately need for his mother became part of his adult personality. It seems that his father's only influence in this problem was the money he left him, which gave him the means to get what he thought he wanted.

The religious commitment likewise found a compromise form—the religion of fellowship. This form began in his early undergraduate days using the heroic material of his childhood and transforming it into an adolescent, latent homosexual vision which partook of the common ideals of Victorian youth. "I have set my heart on our founding a Brotherhood," he wrote; "learn Sir Galahad by heart; he is to be the patron of our order."[44] A few months later, he wrote (to Burne-Jones) that "we must enlist you in this Crusade and Holy Warfare against the age,"[45] to which Mackail adds that "the crusade then definitely including celibacy and conventual life."[46] From such early visions, themselves derived hardly from any gratifying experience of fellowship at home but from his own technique of *differentiating* himself[47] from all the bothersome "fellows," the retreat to medieval knighthood, ironically grows his subsequent commitment to socialism. Fellowship and socialism were not functions of a spontaneous love of fellows, but were compensatory or guilt-motivated commitments growing from his early sense of estrangement from social life. This is what lends them their religious fervor, their monasticism, their implicit celibacy. Socialism was a retreat from the family. As Shaw once observed, "he never discussed his family affairs with me; and I am not sure that he ever discussed them with his family."[48] Mackail judges unequivocally that he "preferred men's to women's society,"[49] while his letters to his wife, from whom he was often separated, contain numerous inquiries about health but a minimum of affection. An obscure but revealing fantasy of Morris's tells that the feelings he did not get from real domestic or social life were those he hoped for in his "religion of fellowship." Bruce Glasier records the fantasy as follows:

> I'll tell you the kind of God I should want my God to be. He'd be a big-hearted, jolly chap, who'd want to see everybody jolly and happy like Himself. He would talk to us about his work, about the seasons and flowers and birds, and so forth, and would say "Gather round, boys, here's plenty of good victuals, and good wine also—come put your hand to and help yourselves, and we'll have a pipe and a song and a merry time together."[50]

The source of justification for this telling little fantasy is the common religious value, the belief in a benevolent God. But as a genuine adaptation, this defense carries little weight. The fantasy shows religion transformed into the whole range of sensual (oral) activities—the pipe, and song, but most of all, the "good victuals and the good wine," which were present in abundance in his home in Woodford, the excess of which, and the necessity for which, now finds their adolescent form in the quest for fellowship, the God who is himself "one of the boys."

Here one sees, at least in rudimentary form, the emotional constituents of Morris's utopian personality. In particular, defenses, following the modes suggested by Houghton, were indeed developed in early childhood, the heroism, Galahad, diligence—the "steadiness and hard work" he later claimed to his mother—a certain kind of monastic "gospel" motivating them, all of which did emerge in an effort to redesign the world. The need for good victuals and wine, the demand for supreme intimacy with physical materials, the entire commitment to the actual fashioning of the object of his love—these are his infantile wish materials. These mark the oral-sensory features of the wish, the need for merging himself totally with his objects.[51] The important point is that the Victorian constellation of his childhood can now be seen as continuous with the wider, external factors fostering the emergence of utopianism in the Transition —the technological threat to Victorian identity. From the beginning, Morris's attempt to define his identity was inhibited by a nagging ambivalence that even in adulthood was never overcome: one foot was always in Kelmscott, the other in socialism.[52] The only domain of unification, created six years before his death, was Nowhere, and this utopia like the many others simply offers a documentary expression, complete with childish fantasy, of an unattainable "feast"[53] at the end and the adolescent adaptive structure of good fellowship. Both Morris's cultural and personal identities were, unfortunately, nowhere.

Although in subtle contrast, Edward Bellamy's identity is more familiarly "utopian," in that he was not as deeply or as manifestly troubled as Morris and was apparently more satisfied with his lot. Nevertheless, the earmark of the utopian personality, the adolescent struggle for identity, is likewise discoverable in him. An interesting polarity suggests how to view the likeness of their personalities. Mackail wrote that Morris

never looked at himself. He had a curious dislike of mirrors. One of the most obvious pecu-
liarities of his house at all times was the absence of mirrors or looking-glasses; there were none
at all in any of the living rooms, and none in his bedroom.[54]

In what seems to be a more important context, Bellamy wrote:

What is my motive in writing at all? Surely chiefly to see myself reflected from the page, to
know myself. Consciously, or subconsciously, this is the motive that impels men to do work
of any sort, to express themselves in speech or written words, or stone or colors or song or
empire building. The woman before the mirror is after all the type of all human behavior.[55]

Morris's idiosyncrasy about mirrors suggests that he sought to repress what
Bellamy aimed to understand consciously—their preoccupations with themselves, preoccupations which ultimately dominated their personalities. Where
Morris's effort to find out who he is emerged in his special intimacy with
objects and the "Brotherhood," Bellamy, in his youth, moved to meet the
problem by verbalizing it in psychologically candid terms. Although Bellamy
was also prone to dreaming up fantasies, the real-life content of these fantasies
was always the dominant element, as opposed to the dominance in Morris of the
mythological. Much as in the above passage, Bellamy *states* what Morris *feels
but represses*, the overall bent of Bellamy's personality tended toward denoting
in conscious, rational terms the same problem that Morris coped with mainly in
expressive, artistic forms.

Yet Bellamy's increased consciousness of what was happening to him did
not finally lead to a life of greater objective accomplishment or fulfillment and
did not transcend the utopian bind. Bellamy's life was unusually sedentary,
showing little travel, some art, and none of the tangible artifacts that Morris was
able to turn out. Consciousness was as much paralyzed by fantasy in Bellamy's
life as fantasy and art were paralyzed by social understanding in Morris. In
other words, the psychological bind in either case is the same; both were arrest-
ed in the incipient stages of identity-formation, an arrest which both men tried
to express and overcome in the utopian vision.

The Victorian defenses operating in Bellamy's childhood, accordingly, are
similar to those in Morris's. Bellamy's son Paul wrote:

When I was a little boy, I found that the one childish game which my father really seemed to
enjoy playing with me was soldier. We used to clear off the dining table, set up the little
images and shoot at them in turn with a spring toy gun which discharged a small wooden
projectile . . . amid a running commentary about Napoleon, whom he considered by all odds
the greatest military genius. . . . I have been greatly puzzled all my life at his military bent, as
it runs counter to all his ideas . . . that no war is worth while.[56]

Rationally, Bellamy's military preoccupation may seem anomolous in itself,
and it was probably responsible for the Industrial Army in *Looking Backward* to
which Morris and others so objected. But his preoccupation is of the same

psychological cloth as Morris's early worship of medieval chivalric heroes.[57] It arose, Arthur Morgan tells us, because Edward's "family of preachers . . . did not entirely meet the craving of a boy whose heroes were warriors and other men of action, so he took great pride in a romantic character . . . Captain Samuel Bellamy, a New England filibuster and pirate."[58] At about 10 years of age, he listed "what I think ought to be the character of a soldier."[59] Morgan's "did not entirely meet the craving" must be a vast understatement, however, in view of the kind of man Bellamy's father was, which is suggested by an anecdote Sylvia Bowman reports about how things went on at the Bellamy dinner table.

> As the Bellamy family sat around the table at meal time, the lads would frequently become so ardently argumentative that the Reverend Bellamy [the father] would summarily end the discussion by banging the table with the handles of his knife and fork and by shouting above the din: "Sing Old Hundred! 'Praise God from Whom all blessings flow . . .' "[60]

The Reverend Rufus King Bellamy was, simply, no gallant hero but a somewhat arbitrary administrator of authority. "One of the most intimate friends of the family said," Bowman reports, "that the four boys valued their mother's opinion more than their father's. Her discipline pervaded the home."[61] Bellamy's mother, her daughter-in-law wrote, "was greatly respected in the community, whereas Father Bellamy was greatly loved."[62] At home, one guesses, authority was not effectively dispensed by the father, who was also, apparently, "extremely fat."[63] His singing and excessive eating suggest the religious orality syndrome, while just the workings of this syndrome in his occupation created an image of the arbitrariness of traditional religion. The young Edward's imagination of more adventuresome, more rebellious figures points to a distinct *opposition* to the things his father stood for, rather than a mere insufficiency of his outlook, while the honorific value of service he saw in the military was a defensive overlay for its rebellious motivation.

Bellamy's mother, who was "respected" in the community, was thus probably the source of this defense, as well as of the fantasy. It was she who was Edward's first motivation for attaching himself to heroic fantasies, so that his fantasies began to have a close association with the source of feminine love. Sylvia Bowman indicates that "the most important aspect of his education was his voluntary reading which his mother so greatly encouraged."

> From the day that he learned his letters, the quiet, earnest boy was an insatiable reader of the biographies of great men and of tales of adventure. As a result of his literary fare, he lived in a dream world in which he aped the actions of his heroes. From the books he read, he formed his ideas of "life and action." . . . from his intercourse with heroes and kings, he had gained a royal air in regarding the common hero.[64]

The interest in the military life was not only a function of fantasy and reading. It was also, ironically, a part of the machinery of kinship with his mother and a covert rebellion against his father. The idea of military service as a defensive adaptation was thus derived from his relationship with his mother and worked against his father. So strong was this early-formed bond that Morgan calls his mother and son, even in Bellamy's adult life, "intellectual and spiritual companions."[65]

This bond subsequently gained a much wider and determining expression. When he was about 28, his mother wrote to him and his brother in Hawaii, "How intense is my longing to have you brought into fellowship with him, Christ."[66] While this wish for "fellowship" is reminiscent of Morris's own "religion of fellowship" and of its key role in utopianism in general, it seems to have been gathering force as part of young Bellamy's thinking considerably before this recorded wish of his mother's. Four years previously, Bellamy had written a small essay called "The Religion of Solidarity," in which he affirmed that "as the Christian believer strives that he may enter into the mystical kingdom of heaven, so also the infinite enlargement of life spoken of awaits only those who strive after it in a like spirit."[67] Though his vision is patently identified with Christianity even as it takes on its Bellamyistic flavor, this flavor, in the absence of the Christian overlay, assumes the old form of the utopian wish for total fusion with the universe.

> There is a conscious solidarity of the universe toward the intuition of which we must struggle, and that it may become to us, not a logical abstraction, but a felt and living fact. As individuals we shall never be complete. The complete man lacks the completion of the rest of the universe. . . . Believe that your sympathy with infinite being, infinite extension, infinite variety, is a pledge of identity.[68]

While it is characteristic of Bellamy to have perceived that this wish of his was connected with his quest for identity, it is equally characteristic that he should have pursued such a fantasy as if it could somehow become a reality. Since his mother played so instrumental a role in the formation of his identity, it is no wonder that the subsequent pursuit of this fantasy, having passed through the stage in *Looking Backward* where the new society is symbolically identified with the reincarnation of Edith Bartlett (his 1887 fiancée) in Edith Leete,[69] who rescues Julian from his nightmare of the "past," winds up in a reverie that resuscitates the infantile terms of the earlier "mirror" fantasy. In "A Positive Romance," published posthumously, the hero finds his own identity in the doctrine that

> In woman humanity is enshrined and made concrete for the homage of man. This is the mighty indwelling which causes her to suggest something more august than herself, and invests her with an impersonal majesty commanding reverence.[70]

The long sought merger with ''humanity'' seems also to be a move toward the same woman from whom Bellamy gleaned his first conscious notions of what humanity really was, his first motives for ''serving.''

Bellamy's first awareness of an identity problem appeared early. ''After at least seven years of interest, almost to the point of infatuation, in a military career,'' Morgan writes, ''failure to be admitted to West Point probably was the greatest blow to his hopes [he] had experienced up to that time.''[71] This failure, it seems, became the archetypal image, for a very long time, of the total failure of his own life. He wrote some time later:

> My case is like that of one nurtured in the belief that he was a prince and a royal heir, feeding his youth on dreams of war and high council, who should at the threshold of manhood suddenly find himself to have been a mere nurse's changeling, a plebian.[72]

The terms ''nurtured'' and ''feeding'' commonly used as they are in this context underscore the feminine—the oral—instrumentality in the creation of his ''manhood.'' The failure, moreover, implies for him a denial of his *maternal* ancestry; his plebian character is the result of his not being his mother's child. In the continuation of the passage in which he questions his motives for writing and sees himself as a ''woman before the mirror,'' he conjectures that he

> must write me a fable of a man that shall present him under the similitude of a genius doomed to walk the earth in banishment, toil, bitterness, misery until he learns the secret of his own shape, and form, and to this and seeking everywhere a mirror and finding only fragments too small or too blurred to render back a full reflection. ''Poor genius, I am sorry for thee, even if thou were not myself.''[73]

In Bellamy's own declaration of his lack of genius, in his fantasy of not being able to *find* the right mirror, the likeness of his psychology with Morris's emerges in the first attempts to replace the lost military career with the literary one. As with Morris, late adolescence was a period of profound disillusionment and self-abnegation, where Bellamy's quest for a modest self-understanding through literature is a direct analogy to Morris's search for pleasurable work in art. Bellamy's temporary experience of, to him, womanly narcissism, of thus *being* the woman he is trying to reach in ''humanity,'' here joins with his motive for writing and thus creates the professional milieu he is to substitute for the lost world of military service and also suggests the ambivalence involved in this choice.

The circumstances surrounding the high point of his career, the creation of *Looking Backward,* suggest vaguely, though significantly, how his response to his father and what he stood for work into this feminine heroic system in his identity problem. The work was written, first of all, about a year after the death of his father. About a month before this death in 1886, Bellamy wrote to his wife: ''that he will in the end kill himself with his knife and fork there is not the slightest doubt, but I hope we may, by constant endeavors, persuade him to postpone his suicide for a few years.''[74] Although, psychoanalytically, there is a kind of standard meaning of such a ''prediction'' by a son of his father's death as a disguised wish for that death, the presumed method of death is more revealing of this particular situation. The knife and fork are what Bellamy's father banged on the table to legislate silence and to overrule the exuberance of the dinner table discussion—and here they are turned back on him as the instruments of his death. These eating implements, furthermore, suggest that the oral battle between Edward and his father, where the son's words were originally conquered by the father's food, now shifts its outcome in favor of the son, such that food as the machinery of his father's death might have seemed to Edward a just revenge. The great nemesis that is conquered in *Looking Backward* is Hunger, so that the son's book itself—in its words—satiates his own hunger, thereby backhandedly identifying with his father but also taking on the heroic stature lost in his early failure experience. In this way, the book seeks to resolve the violent part of his characteristically masculine oedipal condition. It is noteworthy, finally, that his father's death—as a suicide—is presented as a subjective inevitability—''I have not the slightest doubt''—at the hands of the knife and fork, as if to allow it to fulfill a preappointed destiny in the relationship between father and son. In reality, his father's death seems to have caused no trauma for Edward, as he moved into his home afterward and began writing his major work. But these apparently marginal circumstances of the writing suggest that even at age 37 elements of Edward's drive toward some kind of social identity are still seeking an organizing principle.

The only important observable frailty in Bellamy's life seems to have been somatic. Morgan suggests that the ''controlling limitation'' was that ''of personal vigor,''[74] as he was often ill and died prematurely of tuberculosis. Yet, here, perhaps, is the outlet of the energies that the utopian interest could not resolve. At the end of the passage in which he discovers himself a ''plebian,'' Bellamy writes of himself in the third person that ''he could only desire to die,'' and the distance in years between *Looking Backward* and his death is only four more than the corresponding distance between *News from Nowhere* and Morris's death. Both works, it seems, represented for their authors an important emotional finality, a last attempt to create a unity, a coherence, an emotional organization through which their emotional unrest could be at last overcome.

For the emotional finality sought by the utopian fantasy, however, no defense could really be adequate. Like the historical wishes for the new worlds and heavenly kingdoms, the childhood needs of Morris and Bellamy, the emotional problems of the Victorian child and the Transition adult, are in essence not susceptible of the total solution, of the *universal* societal resolution they remorselessly demand. The only fulfillment these needs can hope to achieve is in a context that openly acknowledges that they are only wishes and fantasies.

In an oblique sense, both Bellamy and Morris intuited that this was the case. They tried throughout their lives to formulate, to express their wishes as artistic products. Yet in them—and in many utopias like them—the wish remained too strong to permit a full emotional commitment to the partial worlds of either art or socialism or fellowship or solidarity or nationalism. Moreover, the collective anxiety of the Transition reinforced their continued retention of the wish for ultimate utopian realizability, so that this mutual interaction brought utopian enthusiasm to the highest level in its history.

In the twentieth century, as we have seen, the intellectual justification of utopianism, in the new power gained from science and technology, made peace with the various domains of partial realization. In the Transition, the fantasy understood, so to speak, that it was about to be left unjustified, and this is part of the reason for its great prominence. Caught between the demise of its ancestral fantasy, Christianity, and the diminishment of the intellectual justifications, yet faced with its own permanence in the human personality, the world of art was the only one left to allow the utopian fantasy any social viability at all. This shift to art was what was happening when the utopian fantasy began to affiliate itself in the nineteenth century with the most important of Victorian literary forms, the novel. Psychologically, we recall, the world of art calls for an emotional commitment identical in many important aspects to that required by the religious world, especially the initial act of faith. Connected as it was with the religious impulse, the utopian fantasy, like others of a superstitious or mythological texture, quite naturally began seeking in art a suitably relevant dwelling place. The rejection by both Morris and Bellamy of their religious heritages and their turn, albeit anxious and provisional, to art, acts out this development of the utopian fantasy in the Transition. The novel thus became the new cultural form of the utopian fantasy in the Transition. But this form, like the intellectual one, now appeared inadequate so long as the fantasy insisted on its utopian title.

# 5

# The Novel as an Unsuitable Form

There are no easy answers to the question of exactly how art defines, preserves, and changes cultural identity. Psychoanalysis has raised the question insofar as it views art as the attempt to give permanence to the most important feelings of the culture. Although it is customary to treat art as a manifestation of philosophical, historical, intellectual, and sociological movements, there is no reason to omit from this list the idea of literature as a motivated, affective activity. The value in art is established primarily by a popular desire to enjoy and involve ourselves in it, and only after such attention is paid do the more intellectual views of it gain relevance. If artistic form—the particular group of aesthetic attributes that make it seem "artful"—is considered as a special kind of affective defense, a special way of making feelings available and enjoyable to us, and if this form is demanded on a popular scale, it is fair to conclude that this form constitutes the expression of a key adaptive need of the culture. The relationship between this form and the fantasies that it presents, furthermore, create a paradigm of the "personality" of the age, or, as we have heretofore called it, the identity of the age.

The appearance of the novel on the cultural scene is closely congruent with the appearance of modern science, modern society—and modern utopianism. Like the empirical character of science and its technological results, the singular form of the novel belongs only to the last three or four centuries, and must thus be expressive of collectively held feelings occasioned by the peculiar demands of post-Renaissance modernity. More particularly, a prose story—or tale or saga—between the covers of an easily purchasable book, reachable by increasing percentages of the mass of people, is likely to symbolize the means of cultural self-management common to this age of growing technology and intellectual order. From its early epistolary tales of the middle class, the novel became the main literary genre of the growing ranks of the literate population. Its reassuring power derived from its extending the source of artistic enjoyment into the privacy of the home and the individual mind, although remaining all the while a public experience as well. By sacrificing the need for meter or for actors and a stage, the novel form gave fantasy-life a new latitude and thus underscored the increasing power and importance of private fantasy-life as a response to growing public turbulence—industry, cities, larger wars, empire, and so on. The form acted as a defense by serving as a buffer between the upheavals of the public world and the repression of the private.

Accordingly, the novel became a major literary form of the Victorian age. By making love, marriage, and family their central concern, Victorian novels successfully disguised issues of sexuality and passion with "cleaner" values of loyalty and social order. Both the order of society and the order of the novel coalesced to offer the fantasy-lives of the repressed populace the illusion that all life is as well organized and devoid of sexual complications as it seems to be in childhood. This order was assured by the ideals of hard work and gentlemanly heroism of the chivalric gallant—the Mr. Knightlys and his literary progeny. The increasingly popular utopian fantasy at the beginning of the Transition attached itself to this prevailing form to create the more or less distinct genre of the utopian novel, or, in more theoretical terms, the special combination of feeling and form that comprises Transition utopianism. Sales of utopian novels, statistics show, reached well into the millions; writers of these novels in both England and America were into the hundreds, and more utopian novels were written in the 20 years surrounding the turn of the century than in the 80 years on either side of the turn from 1850 to 1950.[1] The special power of the novel's form dovetailed with the hyperurgency of the fantasy in a massive campaign to achieve utopia at last.

It is, of course, only in retrospect that we see clearly how the campaign failed; there are only a handful of utopian novels remaining in print—and as yet no utopia. During the Transition, utopian novels held the status of popular art, an entire brand of art that is consumed more or less uncritically by large numbers of people, and the difference between the fine and the cheap was blurred. In such suspension of taste, it is as if the discriminatory powers of the individual are temporarily suspended—or perhaps suspended in this one area—so that the safeguarding function of individual taste is displaced onto the condition of collectivity in a public abandonment of judgment. "If everyone else is doing it, it must be good for me too" is the kind of thinking involved here. With the powers of censorship diverted, the fantasy—or the regressive content of the literature—is free to be consciously enjoyed by all, in public and private, so that the process of reading the novels on the societal scale takes on the aspect of a collective religious ritual. But this substitution of a popular disposition for individual taste, as we have seen in other contexts,[2] signals the adoption of adolescent psychology. In any fad-response, a general weakening of a person's discriminatory functions sets in, and this weakening corresponds to the usually temporary casting off of mature standards and the adoption of the more exuberant, but less controlled adolescent standards (as is easily observable in the com-

monness of fads among adolescents). The widespread popular re
utopian novel, we might today claim, reproduced the psychology
historical manifestation of the utopian fantasy. Instead of a mille
tion, the same energies are now cast in symbolic form, though the wish is
the same.

Because the wish was so strong, and because of the need to express so
strong a wish, the formal aspects of utopian novels could be seen as adolescent
as well. Or to put it another way, what one might call mature formal features in
the Victorian novel *became*, in the utopian novel and for the Transition reader,
adolescent features. Robert DeMaria outlines the form as follows: there is

> an imaginary world for us to explore. In order to lead us through [this] world, [there is] a
> guide, a narrator, or a protagonist of some sort. [There is] usually . . . a preliminary section in
> which all the machinery for the explication is adjusted. When we arrive in the utopian world
> we have to be told what it is all about. Then, finally, we have to return to our own ugly world.[3]

Richard Gerber adds that the explication of the utopian world is usually a ''historical account'' that is ''placed in the central part, where the stranger or the
strangers and the utopian wise man or men meet and discuss all the important
questions connected with the subject.''[4] The Victorian novel's frequent topic of
a family functioning in a full society is reproduced in the universal utopian
society and the several interlocutors responding to it. These characters are almost all men, both ''wise men'' and visitors, and the relationship between them
finds the visitor and the utopian working out an accommodation between each
other and between the visitor and the utopia in general. In both Bellamy's and
Morris's utopias, the respective heroes each fall in love with a daughter of
utopia—in Bellamy's case the girl is the actual daughter of the ''wise man,''
Dr. Leete—and this rounds out the adolescently reconstituted oedipal feelings,
for the love, like the best of Victorian loves, is pure in the most utopian of
senses. The young man searching for his utopian identity finds it in the father
that was missing from his actual life. Both Bellamy's and Morris's fathers, we
recall, were the subordinate of the two parents, so that their real-life identities
had been influenced mainly by their mothers. Fulfilling the wish for the masculine identity also retains the pure love that originally sustained them, and this is
''utopian'' in psychoanalytic terms as well. In the nonutopian real world, one
cannot achieve identity without, in some sense, renouncing one's parents, nor
does one win a ''mate'' in a nonsexual way.

The failure of this form to function and grow enough to preserve the utopian novel is, in the final analysis, relative only to the age (in this case, the
present epoch) that studies the genre; in the Transition, it was, of course, no
such failure. Because the facts of adolescence are culturally determined rather
than absolute, however, what we call an adolescent defense may be better
viewed simply as a failure of the work's artistic identity, an inability to appear

artful to us. This more theoretically general tack, as modern criticism of the utopian novel has suggested, will allow us to trace the failure in the later twentieth century to readers' first and necessary condition of artistic response—the suspension of disbelief, the artistic act of faith. Herbert Read writes, for example:

> A "utopia" might well exhibit all the characteristics of pure fantasy, but rarely does so because the writer had some ulterior ... aim ... which distorts his composition, fixes it in space and time, gives it a basis of subjective intolerance.[5]

Marie Berneri similarly complains of a "certain nervousness"[6] when she read in Cabet: "Under the shape of a novel, the *Voyage en Icarie* is a real treatise on morality, philosophy, social and political economy."[7] In each case the "nervousness" and the "subjective intolerance" arise from an immediate perception that a certain "ulterior aim," a world of not-art, so to speak, has entered the world of art, into which the reader has just gestured him or herself. More intellectually put, Ruyer writes:

> L'utopiste, surtout le fabricant d'utopies sociales, emprunte le vehicule de l'experience mentale, mais il l'abandonne arbitrairement. Il saute du vehicle en marche, des qu'il s'aperçoit qu'il risque d'être detourné de la direction qu'il a envie de suivre.[8]

He perceives a kind of arbitrary behavior on the part of the author—or perhaps on the part of the novel—as if it cannot decide exactly which world it is in, and as if the arbitrariness is governed by some egoistic or narcissistic motive on the part of the author. Best and most pointed of all, however, is Victor Dupont's understanding of what is happening here.

> Lorsque l'auteur entre de plain-pied dans le monde fictif, nous éprouvons a son égard, la tradition s'en melant, une sort de ressentiment, l'impression qu'il ne joue pas franc-jeu et qu'il demande à notre imagination un effort supplementaire qui ne lui revenait pas. Lui-même s'étant au debut indument facilité la tache, devra par compensation user de méthodes subtiles pour gagner notre intéres a une fiction que nous sentons de prime abord trop détachée de toute réalité pour lui accorder d'emblée notre assentiment. Au surplus, de telles methodes exigent du lecteur, pour être perçues et pour le rôle qu'on attend d'elles, une intelligence plus vigoureuse et un sens littéraire plus éduqué qu'il n'en faut pour céder a l'attrait d'une relation de voyage imaginaires ou d'un récit d'extraordinares aventures.[9]

The author appears as a barefoot boy whose pretensions to fiction become an aggressive act. Most importantly, in deviously trying to inveigle the reader into a psychic effort beyond what is required for the ordinary suspension of disbelief needed for a mere adventure story, the author *"ne joue pas franc-jeu,"* does not follow the rules of the game. This "game" is made up of the conventions of reading, and they are being destroyed. Psychologically, the gesture of the suspension of disbelief holds a special value to the reader, so that it is not mere annoyance that he or she experiences when the gesture is juggled or asked to be juggled; it is more in the nature of a dangerous violation. Certainly, any reader is psychically *capable* of shifting worlds according to the particular plan offered, especially when, in utopian literature, the shift is not that complex. But when one enters the world of art this first act of "basic trust" carries a correspondingly fundamental psychological importance. The reader expects, so to speak, to be "fed" something good when his or her taste makes an important preliminary choice. What one gets, however, is a number of demands not only to stop eating, but to *give back* some of the "food for thought." This is probably what made Berneri nervous in Cabet's demand of the reader to "read it again, read it often and study it."[10] The juxtaposition of the two kinds of world in the utopian novel amount positively to a serious emotional offense, because the "eating" child does not know to give back *on demand,* but only to take in the "food."

What is worse, the utopian novel seems to make this demand at every turn and in the very smallest details of its formulation, though the ones which come at the outset are of particular importance. Thus, in Stapledon's *Last and First Men,* for example, the novel opens demanding, "pretend that you believe this,"[11] as if the reader had not already made this pretense *unconsciously.* The demand, however, brings the gesture to consciousness and removes it from the primary-process world in which it belongs. More striking, perhaps, is H.G. Wells's introduction to his *A Modern Utopia:*

> There must always be a certain effect of hardness and thinness about Utopian speculations. Their common fault is to be comprehensively jejune. That which is the blood and warmth and reality in life is largely absent; there are no individualities, but only generalized people. In almost every Utopia . . . one sees handsome but characterless buildings, symmetrical and perfect cultivations, and a multitude of people, healthy, happy, beautifully dressed but without any personal distinction. . . . This burdens us with an incurable effect of unreality, and I do not see how it is altogether to be escaped.[12]

Not only his own utopia is being introduced as "an incurable effect of unreality," but "almost every utopia" as well. The fundamental idea of utopianism— of the fantasy perfection and felicity—is denigrated (though honestly) without regard for the most basic convention of reading. The kind of life that is expected in the gesture into unreality is rationally destroyed. Faced with such a warning, what can the artistic act of faith do? It can only decide on its own destruction—a not so desirable effect. A form of this apology, we remember, appeared in More's original *Utopia* and thus began the tradition through which the artistic formulation of utopia opted for its own destruction ever since.

This peculiar habit of undermining the conventional reading pretense is present in the details of a common linguistic habit of the utopian novel.

> A description of a non-existent social system in the future tense or in the conditional would not only be rather clumsy and dull, but the reader would also feel tempted to question the conclu-

sions arrived at. Such conditional statements seem to ask for a refutation since their very grammatical form points to the unreality of the conception in every sentence.[13]

The reader's placing him or herself in the unreal world of fiction is unconsciously a demand for gratification—*now*. The rationality of infantile gratification is not regulated by time. It is *always now,* and it is a conscious ego function to decide whether now is the right time or not. In picking up the book, consciousness has given the signal that fantasies can be given the free play they demand. But if the word-by-word form of the work, the artistic machinery that is supposed to promote this demand, offers conditional rather than factual experience (as would be the case if the past tense were used), this is a work that is not to be psychically trusted. With such a hesitating self-presentation, what faith can the reader have in the work?

What one believes, in confronting a work of art, is not a simple source of psychic nourishment and reassurance. The faith is additionally that this experience has its own means for perpetuating its generosity, that it is an experience which the reader can assimilate and thus reassure his or her adult values that the decision to suspend disbelief was after all a good idea. What a reader sees as defenses of the work of art are allowed to assume certain defensive duties of the conscious personality. In any work of art the presentation of its fantasy in symbolic terms is the first and main reassurance given to the reader by the work. Understandably, if there is anything in these terms that reduces their own symbolic efficacy—such as an introductory apology or their conditional formulation—the reassurance is compromised, as is the final value of the experience.

The devaluation of the reading experience is immediately translated by the reader into a devaluation of the work, with the resulting judgment that such-and-such is a bad book. This judgment is a secondary or defensive act on the part of one's conscious mind. In the immediate reading experience, a *loss* of defense is *not* perceived. What is perceived, rather, is an *excess* of fantasy material. Accordingly, Berneri writes:

> In spite of the fact that these utopian writers [those of the nineteenth century] were no doubt inspired by the highest of motives, one can't help . . . [feeling] bitter even about the love these utopian writers lavished on humanity, for they seem like so many over-affectionate and over-anxious mothers who would kill their sons with attention and kindness rather than let them enjoy one moment of freedom.[14]

The excess of affection and motherly love offered by the unlimited abundance of the utopia is a wish commonly present in the unmeasuring unconscious. What has happened, however, because of the formal convention of apologizing, is that *this wish was allowed into consciousness.* The conscious reader is permitted to experience the wish too clearly for the good of the whole personality. The reader is asked to entertain wishes that since early childhood he or she has been carefully trained to renounce in the process of getting adjusted to reality.

The interest in works of the imagination is one of the techniques of this training, insofar as art is an especially satisfying experience for the complete personality. When a person confronts what he or she judges to be an excessive experience of wishfulness, the threat posed by this excess is hardly arbitrary. It is an offense to one's long-struggled-for machinery of emotional equilibrium, and the psychological disturbance occasioned by such excess is even greater than the consciously articulated annoyance.

While most critical responses limit themselves to the secondary adjusted response of annoyance or "nervousness," Read's sense of "subjective intolerance" finds kindred assent in a few other similarly unabashed expressions of discontent. Robert DeMaria, for example, prefaces his rigorous survey of the utopian novel after 1870 with the remark that "utopian literature is a desert— vast, frighteningly dry, and monotonous."[15] This response, significantly, he finds hard to control, for even in his objective account of the usual form of the utopian novel, selectively quoted earlier, his own feelings cast their evaluation of this form: "We usually have to suffer through a preliminary section in which all the machinery for the explication is adjusted."[16] Even Victor Dupont's generally calm survey of the quality of the utopian novel reaches these extreme proportions:

> il y a differentes sortes d'Utopies, et parmi elles de bonnes, de mediocres, de mauvaises de même qu'il ye a diverses sortes de romans, et à cote des bons, ceux qui le sont moins et ceux sont détestables; ces derniers en majorité.[17]

It is not often in criticism that any work is judged "detestable." The extremism of such responses testifies more to the affective disturbance caused by the works than to any possible "objective" failure since it is not possible to prove that any work of art is objectively bad. DeMaria's metaphor in particular, which converts utopian abundance into a barren and "dry" desert, expresses the psychological repugnance for the withholding of artistic nutrition by utopian literature.

I have suggested elsewhere[18] that such extreme negative responses—but usually any kind of response that rejects a work of literature—represent the defensive action interpolated by one's conscious mind into its experience of the work. This action is a replacement for, and an objection to, the reader's perception of the failure of the work to provide suitable formal defenses. This sense of formal failure—or lack of perceived artfulness—causes the critical rejection of a work. The twentieth century, by and large, has exercised this kind of defensive critical interpolation in its experience of the utopian novel. Transition readers needed to interpolate no such defenses because the fantasy was justified already by the tacit popular agreement on the value of the fantasy thus presented. In the later twentieth century, the individual authority of critical rejection replaced the collective acceptance in the Transition. What we now see as an adolescent and inadequate literary form was then the suitable vehicle for the utopian fantasy. The change in popular psychology from the nineteenth to the twentieth centuries, as outlined in preceding discussions, was acted out in the change in the popular evaluation of these novels that were so important in the Transition, and eliminated the need for the particular combination of fantasy and form of the utopian novel.

Both the utopian fantasy and the novel form continued to exist in the twentieth century, but much more separately than in the Transition. We are familiar with how the novel continued to grow in the twentieth century, but the mode of existence of the utopian fantasy is not as clear. This fantasy was called "utopian" when it appeared in the context of one of its more familiar defenses: the intellectual, the communal, or the fictional. In preutopian times, we remember, the same fantasy was "millenarian" or "Golden Age" or "republican." The isolated fantasy, in other words, being a more or less permanent fact of human psychology, is the name for an emotion or complex of emotions that acquires at least the potential for public emergence from the universal facts of infantile development. It is hard to imagine that there is any human being who does not wish, in some way, to regain the guaranteed abundance and felicity of the first days of his existence. The novel as the artistic justification of utopianism should be understood as unsuitable only in that it did not perpetuate the utopian fantasy in its literary form. Instead, the fantasy, like the Transition period, underwent an important shift into a status less prestigious and important than that of the novel; the novel, through its increasingly subjective concerns, gained ascendancy over the fantasy's demands for realization while still allowing the fantasy's *feelings* full expression. This psychological transition finds an unusually distinct paradigm in the personal lives, the mutual relationship, the respective work, and the larger concepts of culture of H.G. Wells and Henry James. Wells was a British Victorian who failed to make the transition; James an American Victorian who succeeded. The issue that sundered their friendship tells why the failure and why the success.

# Wells and James: Personalities and the Transition of the Utopian Fantasy

It is almost impossible to assign a simple vocational identity to H.G. Wells. He was at first a teacher of science; he received at the last his doctor of science degree. He was a novelist for many years, turning out ten best-selling novels. He was a social organizer and participated in the days of the Fabian Society. He was a historian who wrote the *Outline of History,* and he was a philosopher who delivered addresses to the Oxford Philosophical Society. Yet who Wells is is hard to say, but for our understanding of the utopian fantasy. The action of this fantasy in Wells's life urges his identification as, first and last, a professional utopian. Like the word utopia, the utopian identity is defined by its own absence.

This, of course, is only metaphorically true; psychologically, the picture is considerably clearer. Norman Nicholson observes that

> Wells cherished in his mind two dramatic pictures of his own personality, and one or the other of these is the hero of most of his novels. First there was the idealised figure, often a scientist or a politician or a writer; a man who intends to change the world; a man who was always writing his autobiography. On the other hand there is a figure who looks out through the windows of a draper's shop: a small man, with a little moustache; perhaps middle aged—and with a paunch; a muddled, bewildered, eager, frustrated little man.[1]

The psychological equivalent of an apparent absence of identity is the personality whose identity is not (yet) formed—either the individual is detained in an infantile state, in which case he is psychotic, or much more commonly, he is detained in the adolescent stage where the resultant adult identity is only partially fulfilling and all the possibilities of identity are still only potentialities. The two figures that Nicholson abstracts represent two conflicting provisional identities whose mutual confrontation perpetually inhibited formation of a clear, stable identity. They are, in the first case, the sense of infantile omnipotence and, in the second, the sense of impotence that cannot adequately cope with the pressure of infantile wishes.

In Wells's real-life personality, both of these figures are represented. He was for a long time a hero of Transition youth—and of many a youth even thereafter; he was a prominent and popular man and moved in the most privileged circles of culture. On the other hand he was too often recognized in these same circles as a "bad boy." "There was no malice in his attacks (on civilization)," Shaw wrote at his death. "They were soothed, petted like the screams and tears of a hurt child."[2] Vincent Brome likewise observes that he "sprang unnecessarily to defend himself, became shrilly engaged at the buzz of a gnat."[3] While most personalities can be seen to harbor to some degree such antithetical elements, those in Wells's life proved paralytic, and the clearest demonstration of this paralysis was in his work and main locus of his identity.

The two elements, in this arena, take the form of the artist and the scientist. Brome suggests:

> There is unmistakable evidence that in *Kipps* and *The History of Mr. Polly,* Wells the artist was untroubled by Wells the scientist. It is, again, a considerable token of what might have been if the unfettered artist had surrendered completely to his own genie and let it take possession.[4]

The heroes of *Kipps, Love and Mr. Lewisham, Tono-Bungay,* and *Mr. Polly*— his four best novels—are all projections and creations of the artist: Wells, the spontaneous bad boy, the small man in the draper's shop. Wells was at his most skillful when he created the heroes who represented the most abiding emotional forces of his own personality. Although these novels were begun in the nineties, they were not completed until the first decade of the twentieth century, when Wells had left the phase in which the scientist was the standard hero, his science-fiction or science-fantasy phase during the *fin de siècle* period. The scientist-heroes represented the constellation of his wishes, while the "artist"-heroes represented the realities of his life. Although Bergonzi suggests no connection between Wells's early admiration of his teacher, Thomas Huxley, and the subsequent Frankenstein character of most of his scientist-heroes, it is likely that this real-life image, through the process of introjection into Wells's fantasy-life, was *transformed* according to the needs of the deeper infantile forces acting within him. Bergonzi argues that there is a "fairly close degree of identification between the idealized figure of Nebogipfel [the scientist in *The Chronic Argonauts*] and the young Wells," and that this figure "represented an ideal that was to remain constant with Wells throughout most of his life."[5] The determining features of this figure, however, were not his benevolence, but the more violent and narcissistic impulses that made them "regard their scientific attainments as a means of increasing their personal power."[6] The image of science for young Wells became in his fantasy-life the modern equivalent of the traditional intellectual defense of utopianism, where, in the words of a classic utopist, "knowledge is power." When this motivating image was apparently abandoned, Wells wrote his best novels, achieved his highest popularity, as the quest for power was transferred onto his "real" artistic "small man" and was now formulated by his comic art.

*The History of Mr. Polly*, Gordon Ray claims, is therefore Wells's most "perfectly harmonious and consistent"[7] work of art. The apocalyptic burning of Fishbourne as the turning point in Mr. Polly's fortunes converts him into a comically rendered messianic hero as he saves an old lady from a burning roof. His own life is analogously saved as he has thrown off all the shackles of domestic life and a mercantile vocation and found permanent refuge in the domicile of the fat old innkeeper of the Potwell Inn. Here is the governing fantasy in Wells's life in its most honest form, but translated into the comic idiom. Nicholson notes:

> The apparently "platonic" union with the fat woman, all passion spent, is surely unusual for a man of only thirty-seven. It may be noticed that Wells's men tend to put on weight and grow middle-aged rather early in life.[8]

The fantasy is not that Wells had a secret yen to copulate with fat innkeepers, but a less secret longing for maternal protection and abundance, achievable by the apocalyptic overthrow of reality and of the petty legacy of Low Church bourgeois life. In this novel, and to a large degree in others of this phase, the adult artist in Wells and the infantile artist within achieved the most acceptable balance of fantasy and form of his lifetime.

Unfortunately, however, the adolescent scientist-idealist-intellectual, or some emotional facsimile thereof, was not permanently abandoned in this phase, so that the fantasies and their social forms associated with this aspect of his personality finally gained the ascendancy in his personality. Residual infantile feelings, marshalled by the adolescent wish-image of the scientist-savior, ultimately overrode any realistic system to which it became attached, and created Wells's utopianism. The situation was, as Margaret Cole has written, that *no* instruments of social transformation could fulfill Wells's supervening wishes:

> The Fabian Society was not the only organization to be abandoned in a fury by the most anarchistic of men, who called continually for planning in human affairs, but was constitutionally unable to abide human planners. The Labour Party, the League of Nations, the U.S.S.R.—all came in their turn under his angry ban.[9]

A perusal of his major nonliterary works after the Transition tells the story: *New Worlds for Old* (1908), *The Great State* (1912), *The Outline of History* (1920), *The Salvaging of Civilization* (1921), *The Way to World Peace* (1930), *The Work, Wealth, and Happiness of Mankind* (1931), *The Science of Life* (1931), *World Brain* (1938), *The New World Order* (1940), *The Conquest of Time* (1942). In these 11 titles alone, the word "world" appears in four of them, and in four others some synonym. He actually came to believe, it seems clear, that it was his job to outline history, to salvage civilization, to show the way to world peace, and to bring the new world order.

The adolescent title to all this activity has already been critically presented. Bergonzi has concluded that

> the hollowness and inadequacy of Wells's utopian aspirations are readily apparent, even if we do not see them in the light of subsequent world events. Wells had a temperamental strain of impatience that made him incapable of tolerating the difficulties and problems and disappointments that are inextricably part of the texture of normal life. He wished, in short, for a world where nothing would ever go wrong; or in other words, a world where no one need ever grow up. . . . For all the elaborate apparatus of applied science and social engineering, Wells's utopias are the projection of a radically immature view of human existence.[10]

Wells's utopian personality was more far-reaching than those of Bellamy and Morris because the utopian wish infiltrated his private domestic life. Bellamy and Morris were married and conducted more or less stable family lives; Wells, though married, went through life ever searching for Miss Right, always living in the emotional state of mind of adolescence, searching for its resolution. "Satiation could never occur," writes Brome,

> because . . . he was either looking for the likeness of the mother he never knew, or wreaking vengeance on the mother he had known. At the same profound level of emotional consciousness he was probably trying to reassure himself that he need never again undergo the emotional malnutrition which was said to have haunted his early manhood, leaving him permanently maimed and hungry for something he could not clearly define. . . . By this reckoning he was doomed to become the prey of a passion he could never satisfy and women were for him a constantly renewed, ecstatic hell. Somewhere eternally round the bend lay that full, beautiful promised land where the *passades* would cease and this dreadful demon riding him confront an unpremeditated passion capable of assuaging every fresh pang it produced—only he was doomed never to reach it.[11]

The problem in Bellamy and Morris was probably repressed according to traditional Victorian demands, in Bellamy's case in the ethical worship of all women, and in Morris's in the renunciation of women; only in their utopias do the inner fantasies become more explicit. Bellamy and Morris were Victorians, while Wells was already a product of the Transition. Hence the exact correspondence between the overt psychic features of his personal life and published fantasies. Wells's adolescence already *experienced* what Bellamy and Morris observed in their adult life and protested in their work. Intensifying the adolescent urgency of Wells's struggle, furthermore, was the everpresent onus of class. Being born into lower-class circumstances, the existence of an aristocratic upper class, a cultural and economic elite, was a more potent source for the formation of Wells's idols[12] than it was for either Bellamy or Morris. This class being a reality, moreover, unlike Morris's medieval knights, tended to encourage the sense of possibility of getting to that top, though the intellectual justification of this wish was to try to equalize top and bottom. The utopian compromise between the wish to *be* at the top and the ethical goal of eliminating it was once again localized in the scientific or cultural hero—an elite seeking to make *all* elite. In Wells's life, it can be said that "all occasions" did inform his adolescent personality.

Wells's childhood, like Bellamy's and Morris's, was Victorian, but even more so, because Victorian values seemed to have been institutionalized in his family. The new degree of personal independence sought by Wells's father from the growing repressive force of Victorian mercantile life urged the family life to center increasingly around Wells's pious mother. Wells poignantly describes in his autobiography that she was the epitome of devoted, selfless domestic management; no effort, superstitious and mindless though it was, was ever spared in the service of her family. Brome writes:

> His mother lived in permanent fear of pregnancy, not because the processes of birth alarmed her, but because it meant another mouth to feed. She was a little pink-cheeked woman with a round innocent face, as incapable of original sin as she was of questioning her conviction that the good God would in the fullness of time remember her plight. Half her energies went to sustaining what Wells considered this sham. She repeated all the dogmas, patiently, unendingly. . . . She prayed, Wells said, to Our Savior, Our Father, the Holy Ghost, and many other magnificent abstractions, to bring a little trade, a little money, a little more attention from husband Joe who had a habit of patting her on the head with masculine solidity—"There now, Saddie"—and then going off to hold communion with his own cricketing gods.[13]

Until Wells's puberty, his father was, as well as a tradesman, a quasi-professional cricket player, and this enterprise took him out of the home more than the usual degree. His mother, Wells reports, was the one who taught him the alphabet and numbers until he went to school, so that literacy, as with Bellamy and Morris, was here also strongly associated with his mother. This bond was made even more powerful, Brome suggests, by the death, two years before Wells was born, of his sister Fanny. Wells, whom his mother called "Bertie," was in an important sense a replacement in the eyes of the heart-broken mother, and he thus received redoubled attention from her. In this new attention, however, there was, Wells observed in his autobiography, an element which we might now view as decisive, in conjunction with the larger cultural forces working on his life, in the formation of Wells's overreaching impulse to capture the twentieth century. "It is my conviction," he writes,

> that deep down in my mother's heart something was broken when my sister died two years and more before I was born. Her simple faith was cracked then and its reality spilled away. I got only the forms and phrases of it. I do not think she ever admitted to herself, ever realized consciously, that there was no consolation under heaven for the outrage Fate had done her. . . . My heart she never touched because the virtue had gone out of her.[14]

Psychologically, this explanation has a remarkable cogency, in view of the unequivocal intellectual rejection of religion in Wells's adult life. There can be little question that the death of her daughter was just not explainable by Mrs. Wells's understanding of celestial justice. Naturally, though, the cruelty could never be admitted to consciousness as such; Wells must be correct in adducing that his mother's loss of faith must have been transmitted to him *unconsciously*. Although this could explain Wells's intellectual rejection of religion, it could also explain his incorporation of rationalized religious forms and impulses into his lifestyle—his abiding wish for salvation, his continuing search for the right woman and the right world, his fantastic belief in their attainability—in short, the fantasy motivations of his utopian personality. Dogma or not, his mother's deep affection for and attention to him helped create the fundamental emotional values of his life.

Wells's father, but for his distance from Wells, might well have offset his mother's excesses. But the distant father, as we have seen, was part of the social condition of the age, as it has been since the rise of large-scale industry. An anecdote Wells relates is revealing in this connection. He was taking a walk with his father when he was in his twenties and the latter in his sixties, when his father remarked, "When I was a young man of your age I used to come out here and lie oh! half the night, just looking at the stars."[15] This was a revelation for Wells because "his words opened a great gulf of unsuspected states of mind to me." Reluctant to ask further about this reminiscence, but curious nevertheless, his next "What for" was met with only "Wondering." And then Wells concludes, "I left it at that. One may be curious about one's father, but prying is prohibited."[16] It is significant, first, that his appreciation of his father's capacities did not occur until Wells himself was in his twenties, thus documenting the distance between them throughout his upbringing. Yet here also is Wells's expression of his sense of the forbidden nature of his father's inner personality, "prying is prohibited," a strange conclusion to draw for curiosity on such an apparently innocuous issue. The effect of this conclusion on his life is suggested, though, in his next paragraph:

> But if he could look out of this planet and wonder about the stars, it may be he could also look out of his immediate circumstances and apprehend their triviality by stellar standards. I do not think my mother ever wondered about the stars. God our Father had put them there "for his glory," and that sufficed for her. My father was never at any time in his life, clear and set in that fashion.[17]

It is not clear, from the autobiography at any rate, what his father actually wondered about—and it is not certain that he even wondered about the stars. What is certain, though, is *Wells's own fantasy* about his father. It is likely that it is Wells, and not his father, who views the stars as evidence of his own "triviality." This small passage suggests that Wells created his own image of his father in place of the needed attachment to a real father.[18] This, it seems, is the identical mechanism that operated in Bellamy and Morris, both of whose fathers' absences or weaknesses allowed the sons to create, under the aegis of their mothers' fantasies and aspirations, hero-images to replace these fathers. It therefore appears that the boy's model of masculine achievement gained its grounding in unreality and became the basis for his—their—subsequent failures to establish realistic identities, and allowed, instead, the products of maternal excesses to predominate.

As in Bellamy's case, it is difficult to determine the effect on Wells's identity struggle of the death of these two important people, his parents. It is true in any case that the roots of the problem were established long before. Nevertheless, as with Bellamy's father, Wells's parents died during a pivotal period of his adulthood, his mother in 1905, when *Kipps* and *A Modern Utopia* were published, his father in 1910, when *The History of Mr. Polly* was published, while in between, in 1908, *Tono-Bungay* was created. That is, the period of his parents aging and death saw the creation of Wells's best fiction. It seemed to him, even, that these novels represented the emergence of his real self. Of *Anticipations* (1901), *Mankind in the Making* (1903), and *A Modern Utopia,* he wrote, in 1908:

> They have, I think, made a sort of view-platform of the world for me. If I was to become a novelist of contemporary life, that was what I had to do. . . . I had to define what I stood upon or write of life in a disconnected and inconsistent way. Now it seems to me I may get on to aspects of this great spectacle of life and feeling in which I find myself in terms of individual experience and character.[19]

This was after his mother's but before his father's death. His estrangement with the Fabians, which was going on in this period, even though it may have been a function of his utopian plans, still seemed independent of his career in fiction, as in 1910 *Mr. Polly* was published. But in 1911, already after the death of his father, he wrote *The New Machiavelli,* a novel which, as Margaret Cole reports, contains "the final summing up of his opinion of the Society," and which caricatures the Webbs as "spinning their narrow semi-conspiratorial intrigues."[20] Unlike the comic novels, in other words, this one was driven by a patently extra-fictional purpose, a purpose which from then on dominated his fiction, and actually defictionalized it. Although a causal relationship cannot be definitively established, it seems that the death of his father offers an explicit turning point in the development of Wells's conception of his role in life, as if saying in paradigmatic form, now that father is out of the way, "mother," the world, civilization, and the like is within my grasp, and I need not be occupied with the petty Pollys and the trivialities of father's—his family's—life[21] that these novels caricatured. This would explain, psychologically, why Wells reversed his statement of his life's purpose issued in 1908, before his father died. The utopian fantasy governing his life, was now, at last, released.

That the utopian fantasy, either in the form of Wells's identity or in some wider cultural context, failed to attain any significant credibility in subsequent decades is a familiar fact of modern history. Although history would also tend to suggest that it simply disappeared, psychologically we have seen that such a disappearance is unlikely. A key aspect of Wells's development during the crucial first decade of the twentieth century, moreover, outlines the psychological fate of the fantasy. Wells's relationship with Henry James, while obviously not the only arena for the transition of the utopian fantasy, was, like Wells's own life, both independently paradigmatic of the transition and historically instrumental in it. As personalities, as literary figures, as influences on public taste, as creators of cultural values, both men wielded major authority. The issues that occupied their thoughts—as well as the issue that precipitated their break—were determining ones of the culture in the decade. This last issue in particular, *the role of form in the modern novel,* polarized all the others by objectifying the personal and cultural psychology that each writer wrestled with —both independently and mutually. James's moral and cultural victory in their debate on the issue dealt the decisive defeat to the utopian fantasy.

Although their differences on the function of form in the novel were beyond any ambiguity, the connection between their dispute and the utopian fantasy is more obscure, and is seen more easily in the troubles of their personal relationship, of which this intellectual issue was a symptom. On the surface here too, only the differences are manifest. James, as Edel and Ray have indicated,

> had an easy acceptance of himself and the world; Wells was working hard to make the world accept him. James knew his place and had always known it: he was reconciled to the man-made hierarchies and wielded his pen as if it were a sceptre. Wells carried on his shoulder the invisible chip of inferior social rank in a society where such matters still deeply counted. [22]

These personal differences, however, suggest, in an inverted way, the bone between them in the "underlying anxiety each created for the other."[23] Wells subsequently wrote in his autobiography that "I bothered him and he bothered me."[24] Edel and Ray further observe that "both writers touched deep inner chords within one another, chords of mutual response and of troubled feelings."[25] It is this mutuality, mysterious as it seems, that formed the psychic milieu which worked out the fate of the utopian fantasy; this fantasy had been the original ground of their attraction for each other.

From Edel and Ray's brief juxtaposition of the two men, it is easy to see why James bothered Wells, and why, in particular, James's personality might have been a singular irritant to the gathering force of Wells's utopian aspirations. These aspirations, we know, were born of Wells's indignant perception of his own inferiority, his "triviality." "One suspects," Edel and Ray continue, "that he experienced the American novelist as he experienced the British upper classes: there remained always an underedge of hostility."[26] Psychologi-cally—or unconsciously—this "underedge" was far more violent than its sur-face, as it worked in the service of well-established infantile feelings, them-selves originally unrelated to the upper classes in any direct way. Along with James's affiliation with the upper classes, though, Wells must have perceived the factor of a legislative power that "The Master" held in an "establishment" sort of way, and which worked on Wells in a particularly insidious vein—through James's characteristic indirection, circumlocution, inveterate polite-ness, which, in their role as defenses in James's personality, aggravated Wells's impatience with James's power and added to Wells's experience of its immova-bility. All of this emotion in Wells was expressed as a growing rejection of James's most tenacious professional commitment—the sanctity of form and dis-cipline in the novel. Wells wrote that the novel "had to be kept free from the restriction imposed upon it by the fierce pedantries of those who would define a general form for it;"[27] James held that while the novel "opens such widely different windows of attention; . . . that is just why I like the window so to frame the play and the process."[28] Their difference over art was the same as their difference over life. Wells believed, Desmond McCarthy noted, that life, like art, "was a hold-all into which you can cram anything you have read,"[29] whereas life to James needed the same order, the same decorum, the same sense of system and organization that he created in his art. What is clear then, at least from Edel and Ray's analytical presentation of their relationship, is Wells's impatience and irritation with anything, any force, any principle that seeks to circumscribe his response to life and thus inhibit his utopian personality.

James, meanwhile, did not appear to be bothered in the sense of being irritated or impatient as Wells was. Although Edel and Ray indicate that James was "troubled" by Wells, they are not as explicit about how his *personality* was troubled, but concentrate rather on his more rational perturbation at Wells's unwillingness to learn from him—or from anyone really. There is no indication in their essay, in other words, that James's response to Wells was in any way excessive, that James in any sense perceived Wells as threatening to him, or that there might have been an irrational impulse in James—irrespective of the objective rationality of his criticisms of Wells—to limit, confine, or reduce the emotional importance of the response to life that Wells represented. It is true that there is no explicit evidence to this effect. Yet it is undeniable that a part of James's response to Wells was excessive. This excess suggests the source of the inner trouble—the "bother"—that Wells caused James and thus suggests the common affective ground of their relationship.

Although Edel and Ray indicate that James was attracted to the "alert, sharp mind of the young Wells,"[30] that there was a "fascination of the Master for the young man,"[31] James's letters to him suggest that there was a wider scope to the attraction. Early in their relationship, James wrote to Wells that "you reduce me to mere gelatinous grovel. And the worst of it is that you know so well how. . . . Your spirit is huge, your fascination irresistable, your resources infinite."[32] Some time later, when Wells attained a significant popularity, James wrote, "What am I to say about Kipps but that I am ready, that I am compelled, utterly to *drivel* about him?"[33] Responding some months later to *The Future in America,* he said that "I have done nothing today but thrill and squirm with it and vibrate to it almost feverishly and weep over it almost profusely (this last, I mean, for intensity of mere emotion and interest);" toward the end of the letter, he observes that "I am gripped and captured and overwhelmingly beguiled," signing it "breathlessly yours."[34] And even toward the decline of their relationship, he wrote, responding to *Ann Veronica,* that he is ready to "vibrate to you visibly and audibly under that pressed spring."[35]

If Edel and Ray are correct in observing that to James "Life was a jelly, quivering and formless, and it had to be poured into a mould, given shape and form, if the result was to be finished art,"[36] it can be inferred that Wells's reduction of James to "mere gelatinous grovel" must have meant to the latter an experience of a certain primary level, which constituted life outside the confines of artistic or social decorum. Whether James's response to Wells is denotative or expressive (it certainly seems the latter), the allocation of such superlatives to Wells, juxtaposed to the liquefaction of his own being, attended by the vibrations, the thrills, the squirming, and the profuse weeping, suggest an emotional expressiveness common in children. While it is true that James's criticisms of Wells appeared subtly interwoven with these responses, a fair conclusion to be drawn is that *both* responses and criticism represented important parts of James's total reaction to Wells. Edel and Ray are persuasive in their defense of James's criticism of Wells, but they omit discussion of the excessive nature of James's more emotional responses. Thus, when James cites "just this ability and impulse to simplify—so vividly" in Wells as "what I all yearningly envy"[37] in him, it is clear that the envy is of equal importance to the implicit criticism in the term "simplify." The expansiveness and range of Wells's energy that James delicately criticizes is *reproduced in the letters of response to Wells's work; James himself must at some level of his experience be partaking of the kind of excesses he criticizes in Wells.* In his letters, which obviously represented a part of the world beyond art, there is a relaxation of his usual demands for emotional control, and the resultant emotional self-indulgence emerges alongside the gentlest of rebukes to Wells. The source of the Wellsian "bother" now becomes clearer as a function of James's personality. Although James never admitted it, it seems likely that just as James represented the kind of masterful control that Wells unconsciously aspired to, Wells represented to James the kind of spontaneous emotional abandon—even more—the emotional anarchy, the ability to aggressively display and express very deep and infantile feelings, that James unconsciously harbored within himself, the "gelatinous" nature of which James spent a lifetime controlling in his art. This then is also the source of the *mutual* bother: the desire to express and have the world accept and submit to an infantile desire for omnipotence. As we have seen, this desire overpowered Wells's personality, compromised his identity, and devaluated his work. In James, however, the desire was transformed into a patient search for *formal omnipotence* in art which, in its main defensive capacity, established James's identity as "The Master" of art and subdued the demands of his infantile feelings.

The development of James's relationship to Wells can be characterized from James's viewpoint alone as a gradual overcoming of his own excessive response, which, in terms of his own personality can be stated as the overcoming of his own temptations to excess. On reading Wells's *Twelve Stories and a Dream* in 1904, James wrote:

> Of the little tales in t'other book I read one every night regularly, after going to bed—they had only the defect of hurrying me prematurely to my couch. They were each to me as a substantial coloured sweet or bonbon—one pink, the other crimson, the other a golden amber or a tender green, which I just allowed to *melt* lollipopwise, upon my imaginative tongue. Some of the colours seem to me perhaps prettier than the others, as some oranges are the larger and some the smaller, in any dozen. But I (excuse me!) sucked *all* the oranges.[38]

The sense in which art is a food for emotional consumption, a reward for the initial oral act of faith in it, here enlarges James's early "gelatinous" response to Wells. Just as he earlier melted, the candies now *"melt"* on his own "tongue" as he "sucks" them *"all."* While the apology for totally incorporating them, apparently uncritically, is obviously a joking allusion to the totalistic impulses of the mischievously greedy child, it is no joke in the unconscious psychological sense. Reading in general, and Wells in particular, especially as they have gained singular priority for James's discriminating though still omnivorous tastes, further indulge these impulses, this time in the sweets metaphor that he so carefully controlled in his art. Yet this control resumed with respect to Wells as their relationship deteriorated, though the control reveals a significant feature. Writing of Wells and Bennett in 1914, he said: "They squeeze out to the utmost the plump and more or less juicy orange of a particular acquainted state and let their affirmation of energy, however directed or undirected, constitute for them the 'treatment' of the theme."[39] Although the critical ballast of this judgment is unequivocal, the image of the orange returns, juice and all, but now with the implication that this orange is no longer available to him. James was not one to openly express any bitterness, but in view of what such oranges meant to him—the orange of a "particular acquainted state"—the fruits of consciousness, one cannot avoid sensing a touch of bitterness and anger at his failure to win, with all the complimentary wiles of his personality, the fruit of Wells's artistic deference.

Thus, an aggressive component emerges in James's need to eat of Wells's sweets, a component present even at the early phases of their acquaintance. Having read in 1902 Wells's *Two Men*, James replied:

> It is, the whole thing, stupendous, but do you know what the main effect of it was on my cheeky consciousness? To make me sigh, on some such occasion, to collaborate with you, to intervene in the interest of—well, I scarce know what to call it: I must wait to find the right name when we meet. You can so easily avenge yourself by collaboration with *me!* Our mixture *would,* I think, be effective. I hope you are thinking of doing Mars—in some detail. Let me be *there,* at the right moment—or in other words at an early stage.[40]

It is not the usual state of affairs for James to be at a loss for words, and it is even less likely that James, in view of his impenetrably personal attachment to his work, would actually lend his name to a collaborated work of fiction. I can only surmise that James knew what he had in mind but could not find a word sufficiently delicate to say that he wanted to be there at the outset of the new work so that he could *discipline* it, and thus offered Wells a kind of consolation in the imagined prospect of vengeance for James's imminent artistic restrictions. The prospect of collaboration merges two aspects of James's incorporative impulse—the desire to himself enjoy Wells's energy and exuberance and the desire to *bring it under his own artistic dominion.*

This latter wish is the cause of James's view of his own consciousness as "cheeky," for James tried to do with his consciousness, his artistic skill, what he thought Wells was doing with his envied unconsciousness, his undisciplined impulses—incorporate *all* of life's experience. The same adjective occurs in James's response to Wells's utopian visions.

> It is the quality of your intellect that primarily (in the Utopia) obsesses me and reduces me—to that degree that even the colossal dimensions of your Cheek (pardon the term that I don't in the least invidiously apply) fails to break the spell. Indeed your Cheek is positively the very sign and stamp of your genius, valuable to-day, as you possess it, beyond any other instrument or vehicle so that when I say it doesn't break the charm, I probably mean that it largely constitutes it, or constitutes the force: which is the force of an irony that no one else among us begins to have—so that we are starving . . . for a sacred satirist . . . and you come admirably to save us. . . . Cheeky, cheeky, cheeky, is *any* young man from Sandgate's offered plan for the life of Man, but so far from thinking that a disqualification of your book, I think it is what positively makes the performance heroic. I hold, with you, that it is only by our each contributing Utopias (the cheekier the better) that anything will come.[41]

In a typical Jamesian "ambiguity," the genuinely critical part of the response is imperceptibly aligned with the celebrating part. Wells's intellect "reduces" him; the bulk of his response is to Wells's "Cheek," that is, his boyish arrogance that both permitted and promoted his "plan for the life of Man." The criticism, centering in the words "invidious" and "disqualification," is surrounded by denials of their applicability, so that James's own cheeky consciousness here defends what his artistic intuition sensed to be true, namely that cheek is invidious to and does disqualify art. The dominating repetition of the word "cheek" suggests that a deep emotional resource in James has been stimulated by the feeling represented by the term. He notes in particular that it is characterized by a "force" whose singular value is that "no one else among us begins to have" it, and that the rest of "us" are "starving" for it, while Wells has come to "save us." Once again, from the critical viewpoint, the value of this judgment is stable and unspectacular; yet the coordinate extremism of the terminology, divorced of its metaphorical function, defines its unconscious emotional purpose. At some deep level of his experience, James must indeed have perceived Wells as the salvationary being that Wells cheekily claims to be. James was able to make this perception because he *was beset by the identical inner claim,* which his own personality, owing to its specific features, heroically managed to put into the service of his art. Insofar as Wells represented to him, in the "colossal dimensions" of Cheek, a vicarious embodiment of himself, James found him attractive enough to "weep profusely" over and to celebrate so extremely in his epistolary excitement. Yet it must also be true that James's artistic standard, his commitment to right and wrong in art, could permit him no truck with Wells's attitude; most of all with that attitude as it operated in his own personality, so that Wells became to him a projection of that part of himself he was trying to control. Because James was out to save himself, it must have vaguely appeared to Wells that he aimed to do with Wells what he was all along doing with himself. Wells did not ask James to change his work, as James asked of Wells. While Wells's problem was that he could tolerate no direction at all, he also correctly perceived the excess in James's intention toward him. The intersection of their respective problems, in their obverse identity, inhibited productive communication and mutual advance, and their relationship was crippled at the level of passive response to each other's work.

The end of their relationship saw the reemergence—or the mutual assertion, in any case—of the main forces in their personalities. Wells cruelly but pointedly satirized James's elaborate style—with the "irony that no one else among us begins to have"—while James broke the relationship and pronounced Wells in the various aspects of his intransigence "absolutely immovable."[42] Wells, in other words, penetrated the boundaries of social form and plain personal consideration with his uncontrollable "force" and brazenly left a copy of the satire for James. James, meanwhile, invoking his lifetime standards of artistic discipline, simply rued the fact that productive communication could not take place between the two and left it at that. Edel and Ray seem correct in portraying James as having retained a far greater degree of ethical dignity in the matter, and victory for James can justly be claimed on this personal level.

Yet this victory raises further issues. It was, first of all, emblematic of a climactic victory in James's personal life, over the forces of "Cheek" in his own personality, his own vague misgivings that though he had firmly renounced claims on the outside world, he still entertained the wish to capture it. Art and form kept their primary place in his life. Second, art and form also were the victors as cultural wishes, as Wells slowly learned through his continuing frustrations and the ineffectuality of his work in any context. The utopian wish-fantasy was removed from the domain of cultural seriousness as the novel continued its development toward more powerful forms—forms that were clearly descendants of James's hard-won discoveries of the novel's artistic possibilities. James's "victory" over Wells is therefore also reduction of the utopian fantasy by the form of the novel. It can be seen from James's many responses to Wells, that he, almost as naively as Wells created his visions, applauded and encouraged them, and was especially taken with their "intelligence." It cannot be too farfetched to think that when James endorsed "our each contributing Utopias," he viewed his own work as a metaphorical utopia that contributed at least equally to the "anything" that "will come." But this is just the point of transition; once some other form, in this case the controlling work of James's art, became the *metaphor* for utopia, utopia as a word and a concept lost its own formal-defensive status—and this status is what disappeared. The fantasy, in its new artistic form, was unrecognizable as utopia. James's identity as an artist overtook the utopian fantasy from Wells's identity as a utopian.

James did not, of course, acquire the fantasy from Wells, even though their relationship acts out how it was transformed. As with Wells—and Bellamy and Morris—the fantasy was generated in the growth of James's personality and the struggles it had to overcome, struggles which, as with the others, were defined by the emotional ethos of the age. What is distinct about James's life is that, from its very beginnings, it was able to develop an exceptionally successful adaptive capacity. In its larger structure, James's family situation was not unlike the others, featuring a stronger mother, a weaker father who was himself struggling for an identity, and a significant number of siblings. Furthermore, this family likewise posed a formidable challenge to the child aiming to develop from it a secure sense of self. Yet ultimately the identity was won, and its achievement was patently fulfilling. The fantasy over which it prevailed, however, was, in its psychological structure, the same as the one which prevailed over the identity of the others.

The cornerstone of James's adaptive capacities was his ability to *renounce and introject*. Early in life James learned to mediate between reality and his emotional needs by renouncing a vital or morally compelling—though severely problematical—domain of public life, yet creating an increment of personal identity from an *introjected form* of what he renounced. When James was able to create an inner subjective correlative of the renounced object, an essentially stable, untroubled sense of self was the result, accompanied, albeit, by a vague feeling of sacrifice or pain. When introjected, the renounced item became the object of a wish-fantasy that was then reprojected in and passionately held by an artistic structure. In this way James's identity as an artist managed, in a culturally unimpeachable mode, to control his most powerful wishes and become the absolute master of reality. By the end of his life, he seems actually to have felt this mastery, for looking back, he marvels at "the wonder of consciousness in everything"[43] that he then enjoyed. This supreme achievement, this long coveted sense of subjective omnipotence, was secured through an arduous development on both sides of the turning century, culminating in *The Golden Bowl*—"The best book, I seem to conceive, that I have ever done."[44] In this work his heroine claims that "we can have got everything, and kept everything, and yet not be proud,"[45] a development which recapitulates James's lifelong artistic battle with some of his most powerful fantasies, and which ends in this triumph for James, for the novel, for art, and with a new cultural status for the utopian fantasy.

Not surprisingly, this climactic phase began in about 1890, when the culture was already restless. At this point, after having enjoyed two decades of financial and popular success, James's work began to fail in the marketplace. The artistic identity he had thus far built up, largely in the Victorian idiom, was now being called into question. Other problems entered the picture. In 1892, his sister Alice died of cancer, and in 1894, his most intimate known woman friend, Constance Fenimore Woolson, apparently committed suicide, possibly because of James's confirmed independence of her. His identity as an author and as a man threatened from all sides, his response was in two directions. The first was to try the theater—the outside world, so to speak—in order to regain an audience and to acknowledge changing tastes. *Guy Domville,* however, failed catastrophically in 1895, which of course brought on new doubts. The second more encompassing reaction was his intensified work on his so-called "ghostly tales," 13 of which were composed between 1890 and 1903, and in which all kinds of ghosts and alter egos seem to converge on the anxious heroes.

James made a revealing comment about two of these tales, "The Altar of the Dead," and "The Great Good Place." They are, he said, the kind of "things one wants to write all one's life, but one's artist's conscience prevents one. . . . And then perhaps one allows oneself."[46] Exactly why James "allowed" himself to write "The Altar of the Dead" is amply explained by Edel in terms of James's detachment from Miss Woolson and of her unnatural death. "The Great Good Place," however, is more patently concerned with the struggle for artistic identity. The hero's name, Dane, Edel discovered,[47] is also the name of the hall at Harvard where James recorded, late in life, that he had made what is probably the most important professional decision of his life—the decision to renounce the study of law and to become a writer. Apropos, Edel also indicates,[48] that Guy Domville has the same initials as George Dane and goes through a similar experience of renunciation of the outer and retreat to the inner world. The fact that Dane, the writer, is plagued at the beginning of the story by a "continued disposition not to touch"[49] all this literary work matches James's own contemporary disillusionment with his work. The young writer—perhaps an emblem of James's younger, more successful self—waiting to visit Dane only underscores the latter's agitation. Moreover, Dane's valet, Brown, is so annoying with his frequent reminders about Dane's literary obligations that Dane even threatens to kill him. Nonetheless, Dane is able to get away from it all in a dream of a monastery and the pleasant conversation of the good "Brother." As the talk turns to the search for a name for the "great good place," the two men "sat there as innocently as small boys," and as Edel has detailed,[50] the naming process moves from hotel, to club, to kindergarten, until Dane finally offers "babes at the breast," which they both complete with "some great mild invisible mother . . . whose lap's the whole valley" and whose "bosom . . . [is] the noble eminence of our hill."[51] Having thus met the "Great Want," Dane shakes hands with the Brother but in so doing wonders why "in the act of separation his own hand was so long retained."[52] On waking he sees that "it was verily Brown who possessed his hand."[53] This identification of Brown and the Brother leads to the motivating fantasy of the story. Brown, whose life Dane threatened before the dream, is *introjected* as the mild Brother who is sharing the "breast" with him. The subjective act of dreaming both gets Dane to the breast and subdues Brown, while the visiting young writer takes care of his work for him. The wish of the story is as much to shake hands with—"touch" —Brown and the world of literary responsibility he represents as it is to find a name for—subjectively touch—the "great mild invisible mother." Indeed, these two acts form parts of a single feeling. I suggest that the tale troubled James's "artistic conscience" because he dimly perceived too great a psychological correspondence between the tale and the condition of his emotional life at the time. (The same would hold for "The Altar of the Dead.")

The compositional history of *The Golden Bowl,* meanwhile, which began in this period, acts out James's renunciation of the—to him—questionable activities in the "outer" world of the theater and the ghost-story marketplaces, his introjection of its materials, and thus his first step in overcoming this crisis phase. The first recording of the novel's idea was late in 1892, when it was conceived as a short story about the "pathetic simplicity and good faith of the father and daughter in their abandonment."[54] Just before this entry he noted the growing estrangement between men and women in America as a result of the feverish process of wealth-gathering. Clearly, at this point, James himself was estranged from his usual work since he was busy gathering "wealth" in the theater. It is understandable, then, why James would be taken with a tale of "abandoned" Americans, good faith and all. For about 30 months after this, no reference to the tale appears, while during this period Alice and Fenimore died, his play was a disaster, and the first notes were entered for *The Turn of the Screw*, that most ghostly of ghost stories. In early 1895, then, as he is thinking about *The Wings of the Dove*—also a tale of painful abandonment—"in my path" is the idea that has "lain there untouched" since 1892. Soon he records, "the mere touching of it makes my fingers itch," and then, "For God's sake let me try: I want to plunge into it."[55]

George Dane's "continued disposition not to touch" his journals and seals now extends its metaphorical relevance. As James's attention is drawn to the tale, he asks himself if he should not write a "full scenario" of it. But now, a remarkable experience takes place.

> With the utterance of that word [scenario] so charged with memories and pains, something seems to open out before me, and at the same time to press upon me with extraordinary tenderness of embrace. Compensations and solutions seem to stand there with open arms for me. . . . Has a *part* of all this wasted passion . . . (of the last 5 years) been simply the precious lesson . . . *of the singular value for a narrative plan too* . . . of the divine principle of the Scenario? . . . This exquisite truth . . . is a key that, working in the same general way fits the complicated chambers of both the dramatic and narrative lock. . . . The long figuring out, the patient, passionate little *cahier* becomes the *mot de l'enigme*, the thing to live by. Let me commemorate here such a portentous little discovery.[56]

A "divine principle" now presses upon him with the "extraordinary tenderness of embrace" and awaits him with "open arms." In his "plunge" James has made a sudden, unexpected contact of the most important kind. Isn't this physical proximity of the divine identical to George Dane's experience at the monastery? James moves here like Dane, from embrace to discovery. What embraces him is the outer experience of the theater, which has been *introjected* via his private, "patient, passionate little *cahier*" into his main internal world of fiction, and this *"cahier"* is recognized as "the thing to live by." The scenario, as a kind of symbol of the five years of suffering and estrangement in the outer world, is now converted into the "precious lesson." The original *tale* of abandonment, now conceived of as novella length, is given a major development boost, as the *fact* of James's personal abandonment is dealt a decisive blow by the dramatic notebook rediscovery of the scenario. As we know, the tale incubates for another eight or nine years, but much as Maggie Verver ultimately conquers her own abandonment with a portentous discovery, James finally and grandly overcomes the malaise of his "artistic conscience," writing to his agent that the first 200,000 words of *The Golden Bowl* are of the "rarest perfection."[57]

As quiet and private as James's conquests by introjection seem to be, they are, as we might guess, attended by a considerable sense of violence as well as a vague residual pain. Two aspects of James's life, a real event and a dream, help to locate this violence in his personality. The real event was an injury sustained fighting a stable fire in 1861, at a time when he was considering service in the Civil War. Accepting Edel's argument that the injury was not sexual, but remembering that a residual backache stayed with him the rest of his life, the events takes on *symbolic* value for James. Stable fires, as Edel indicates,[58] already held a special meaning in the James family; it was in a stable fire that the elder Henry James lost his leg. In a psychological sense, then, stable fires may have something to do with tests of manhood. The younger James subsequently called his injury a "vast visitation." This name, Edel continues,[59] bears a marked resemblance to the elder James's "vastation," the deep personal denouement he suddenly underwent, under Swedenborgian influence, when the younger James was a year old. The correspondence between the painful events of his own life and the painful events and similar name for them in his father's suggests that images and fantasies of violence were introjected forms of the violence (perhaps even a sense of castration) he seemed to associate with the process of identifying himself as a man like his father. Perhaps because of his pain, James waited until after his father's death to drop the "junior" from his signature.[60]

Consider, finally, what James called "the most appalling yet most admirable nightmare of my life."[61] In this dream, recorded in old age, experienced in adulthood, and set during puberty, the sleeping boy is suddenly confronted with a "visitant" threatening from without his door. "Appalled," Henry overcomes the intruder by pushing the door outward; his own "straight aggression" and "dire intention," however, were "probably still more appalling than the awful agent," as the latter becomes "but a diminished spot in the long perspective, the tremendous, glorious hall" through which "he sped for *his* life." In the dream, the violence and fear vaguely associated with his real-life "visitation" is manifest. He is truly surprised at his own surpassing aggressive "intention," an intention here apparently in the service of self-preservation. This action, moreover, can be viewed as having two aims. The first is the conquest of the intruder, who, Edel's documentation suggests,[62] behaves much as Henry perceived his brother William to behave; the latter always appeared to Henry unapproachably ahead or around some distant forward corner. The "long perspective," "to the wonder of my final recognition," James writes, was the Galerie d'Apollon in Paris, Henry's first visit to which did in fact take place with his brother William. This gallery informs the second aim of Henry's action. Just before his account of the dream, James tells how "those magnificent parts of the great gallery . . . arched over us in the wonder of their endless golden riot and relief," while the whole arena seemed like a "prodigious tube or tunnel through which I inhaled little by little."[63] The assertion of self here is also the taking command of this supreme gallery.

But what does this gallery mean? The fact that he envisions himself in a "tube or tunnel" with breathing difficulty while the hall "arched over" him reminds me that when his mother died, he called her the "keystone of the arch."[64] This, in turn, reminds me that one of his presumably noblest, most admired heroines is named Isabel Archer. In the context of Edel's account of James's relationship with his mother, these topically unrelated correspondences begin to cohere. The main point of the account is that Henry obtained his mother's love by his own ability to withdraw to his fantasies and help preserve the quiet his mother demanded at home. He thus became an observer; mother's love meant for him observation of, rather than participation in, the social doings of the household. His home became a kind of picture for him, which he dealt with by *introjecting* it into his fantasy life. Not only does this fact suggest why there are so many observers in James's novels, why so much dramatic action is seeing, but it also suggests the source of James's lifelong fascination with visual art, with the artistic process itself, and his uncompromising insistence on form and discipline. His introjection of the gallery is subjective capture of home and mother.

Perhaps some of the threads in James's basic tapestry of fantasy and self-management can now be drawn together. An analogy can be made between the monastery, the museum, and his mother, Mary, where the former two are introjected forms of the latter. There is a further analogy between Brown, the Brother, the visitant, William, and Henry Senior, where the former three are introjected forms of the latter two. Introjection of masculine figures involves conquering or subordinating them, which creates for Henry a strong sense of self or identity. The spoils of his victory are the undisputed authority over the museum—the world of art—visual, literary, or feminine. The cost of the victory—the residual backache, the guilt, or the disturbing awareness of his own aggressive power—however high, is worth it and possibly unavoidable because, after all, what the Prince observes to Maggie at the end of *The Golden Bowl* is probably true: "Everything's terrible, *cara*—in the heart of man."[65] The ultimate reward, in any case, is to be able to "touch" his journals and stories. One did not really need or want actual women, for the "embrace" and "open arms" of the introjected women cannot deny him their love. It is fairly clear, then, how the genesis of *The Golden Bowl* partakes of this psychological configuration. It was one of the events in this crucial period of James's life that helped exorcise his "ghosts"—the uncertainties of artistic selfhood, the adverse rivalry from the outside world, the theater, the marketplace. That is why, when he abandoned that long "ghostly" novel, *The Sense of the Past*, he remarked that he would now turn to things "of an altogether human order,"[66] his primary work in artistic fiction.

In James's return to the human order, the train of his personal development merged with the development of the novel in general. With Dostoevsky, as Edel has suggested,[67] James brought on the twentieth-century novel by initiating its "inward turn." James's early impulse to deal with reality from one or another subjective "point of view," in operation throughout his literary career, reaches its most distinct and compelling form in *The Golden Bowl*. These two developments—James's and the novel's—met, in the opening decade of the twentieth century, the larger cultural struggle of the Transition with its utopian wishes. As we have seen, there was an antipathy between the defensive character of James's concerns and the exuberant impulses of the threatened culture, though James's concerns ultimately prevailed.

While obviously no single moment can be selected as the exact point of transition, the year 1905, in which Wells published *A Modern Utopia* and James published *The Golden Bowl*, seems to encapsulate the cultural shift. For both men, these works represented milestones. Although Wells deemed his work an end to a certain phase of his development, it was, ironically, only the beginning of a long and frustrating concluding half of his lifetime. And although James's work was to him the apotheosis of his life's efforts, it was also the beginning of a new domain of fictional art. *A Modern Utopia*, therefore, presents the utopian fantasy in, so to speak, first and last terms, while *The Golden Bowl* defines its new terms. To say a "utopian" fantasy describes James's novel is, admittedly, unusual. Yet in view of what the fantasy represents psychologically, and in view of its pervasive role in that particular period of history when James himself was redefining his artistic identity in partial response to this fantasy, and in view, finally, of its manifestation in James's personality as the key feature of his reaction to Wells, it should be surprising if the fantasy were *not* to be found in the novel. Wells sought to present the fantasy in the combined dress of a traditional intellectual purpose and a more recent artistic one. He aimed at once for the most persuasive of rationalities and the most compelling of imaginative visions. James, on the other hand, intuited the deep inner springs of the fantasy, and, in concert with his life-habits of self-control, renounced all of its claims on reality. Instead, he transferred all the energy of the fantasy, all its emotional influence, to the aegis of artistic control, so that the fantasy in the novel is discernable only as a kind of unconscious emotional theme, a force underneath the work's more literal issues. That the fantasy may actually be seen in both novels, and that Wells's treatment is adolescent and James's adult, however, is discoverable only from a close view of the novels.

# A *Modern Utopia:* Utopian Fantasy and Adolescent Identity

An element in Wells's sense of self, his recognition that there may be stellar dimensions in his own father's personality and, as a result, in his own, helps to motivate the writing of *A Modern Utopia;* it is the element that enables the linkage of the literary, the biographical, and the cultural into the same framework of understanding. The previously discussed passage in his autobiography works out the replacement of his mother's cosmology by his father's, a substitution of stars for God as the heavenly principle. The adoption of his father's cosmology, however, was incomplete, we recall, because it was only an *imagined* dimension of insight that Wells *projected* onto his father. This incompleteness marks the adolescent cast of Wells's personality. Wells's immediate association of his mother to his father suggests that his sense of maternal abundance and totality is the feeling motivating the projection of idealism and depth onto his father. This association thereby defines the source of Wells's protracted vocational ambivalence: a vision of heroism and transcendence, ostensibly in masculine form, but ultimately motivated by the infantile wish for maternal protection. This, we recognize, is the psychological configuration of utopianism that I have explored in several other contexts.

In the novel itself two items signal the activity of this configuration. At the beginning of the work, the modern utopia is located as a planet "out beyond Sirius, far in the deeps of space, beyond the flight of a cannon ball flying for a billion years."[1] To this planet, the narrator—the Voice—subsequently explains, one travels "by an act of imagination" (133), perhaps as the young Wells got there after listening to his father's reminiscence. As in the autobiographical report, the act of transcendence is followed by an association of a more passive and regressive domain of experience. The Voice finds himself on the "neck" and "shoulder" of the Lucendro Pass, where, he remembers, "once I lunched and talked very pleasantly" (14). Since the modern utopia is actually created right on the spot—"suppose that we were indeed so translated" (13)—the presentation of the planet, which is the subject of this initial "topographical" section of the novel, reproduces, in Voice's observations, a process in the development of Wells's sense of self which utilized the incomplete paternal identification to gratify an earlier need for maternal nourishment.

The germinating fantasy achieves its status at the emergence of the samurai, who form the totality of utopian authority.[2] At the "heart of all his explanations," the samurai "tried to make his religion clear to me" (299).[3] The "heart" of this religion is a seven-day sojourn in the wilderness, two features of which are familiar from Wells's biography. "I remember that one night," the samurai reports, "I sat up and told the rascal stars very earnestly how they should not escape us in the end" (307–308). This Wellsian theme of celestial conquest is once again motivated, however, by the similarly familiar Wellsian wish: "We civilized men," the samurai explained, "go back to the stark Mother that so many of us would have forgotten" (304) were it not for the Rule. Much as Wells's association to his mother is framed by a pejorative comparison with his father, the analogous wish to return to the "stark Mother" is disguised by its presentation as a compulsory act of personal discipline. The wish is translated onto a masculine system of values. In this translation, the features of Wells's personality, of the work's style—"the will and motives at the centre" (299)—and the original religious sources of the utopian fantasy all converge.

The idea of a return to the stark Mother, the samurai observes, was the result of a long search: "Many things had been suggested, swordplay and tests that verged on torture, climbing in giddy places and the like, before this was chosen" (303). In the feudal tradition of the samurai, and in the tradition of the Knights Templar, of whom they gratifyingly remind the Voice (174), the sojourn with the stark Mother is recognizable as an adolescent initiation rite. The stark identity achieved by such rites, that of sheer manhood, is likewise sought regularly by the samurai: "I'm only sure of being a man after the second night" (306). In the youthful struggle for manhood, characteristically, two forces are battling. One is the aim to see "how near men might come then to the high distances of God" (310). Like Wells's fantasy father, "I [the samurai] lie awake and stare at the stars" (306). But soon "the stars in the later days of the journey—brought me near weeping" (306), and as the days pass "there are hours when one is just exploring the wilderness like a child" (308), until, in old age the samurai "was found dead in his boat . . . lying like a child asleep" (309). At death, after a lifetime struggle for identity between the god and the child, the child prevails to enshrine the eternal heroic adolescence of the samurai.

The samurai, in addition to having been themselves consistently identified with most public conceptions of Wells's utopianism, in addition to their having retained in Wells's own thinking a determining role even while he renounced the attempt to turn the Fabian Society into a sect of samurai,[4] and in their literary capacity of occupying the longest, most important chapter in the novel, operate as the *object of self-identification for the Voice*. The only dramatic interaction between the Voice and the ordinary utopian population he created occurs through the process by which he identifies himself in the utopian world, and this same process brings him to meet the samurai. The Voice's first encounter with the samurai is when one of them overtakes the supervision of the former's fingerprinting. But while the supervisor insists that the Voice is identical with his samurai double, the Voice's greater certainty of his own "identity" at this point, derived as it is from his trip through the stars, gains the ascendancy, even over the samurai: "Sooner or later," the Voice predicts, "you will have to believe there are two of us with the same thumb-mark. I won't trouble you with any apparent nonsense about other planets and so forth again. Here I am" (169). Subsequently, just before the Voice meets his samurai double, that is, just before announcing his true place in utopia, the duplication is offered as the motive for the trip. The Voice reflects:

> The idea grows in my mind that after all this is the "someone" I am seeking, this Utopian self of mine. . . . His training will be different, his mental content different. But between us there will be a strange link of essential identity, a sympathy, an understanding. I find the thing rising suddenly to a preponderance in my mind. . . . That I have come to Utopia is the lesser thing now; the greater is that I have to meet myself (229).

The meeting of "myself" and the discovery of his "essential identity" supersedes the search for utopia, which is now, at the climax of the work, the "lesser thing." Confronting his double, "the whole fabric of that other universe sways for a moment as I come into his room" (247). Ultimately the excellence of this "better self," his greater height, his "younger" and "sounder" looks, his fewer illnesses, and "better face," weaken this universe by resuscitating another:

> I have stirred up the stagnations of my own emotional life, that pride that has slumbered, the hopes and disappointments that have not troubled me for years. There are things that happened to me in my adolescence that no discipline or reason will ever bring to a just proportion for me, the first humiliations I was made to suffer, the waste of all the fine irrecoverable loyalties and passions of my youth. The dull base caste of my little personal tragicomedy—I have ostensibly forgiven, I have for the most part forgotten—and yet when I recall them I hate each actor still. Whenever it comes into my mind—I do my best to prevent it—there it is, and these detestable people blot out the stars for me (254).

Adolescence was more than a period of humiliation; the damage, rather, was permanent. Like the loyalties and the passions, justice is "irrecoverable," and the early injury to the Voice's identity has then finally blotted "out the stars," which are now available only to "my better self." The Voice's quest for identity, and finally the utopian success of the quest, exposes its essential failure, its (his?) absence of identity. The initial earthly adolescent utopian quest for possession of the stars is undermined by consciousness of the motivation of this quest.

The prevailing world of the Voice in utopia is not the samurai, but the "dull, base caste of my little personal tragicomedy," which cancels all stellar concerns. The population of utopia is divided into four classes—Poietic, Kinetic, the Dull, and the Base. Though "unlike all other privileged castes the world has seen" (299), the Common Rule of the samurai "aims to exclude the dull and the base altogether" (279), while cultivating the more imaginative and diligent Poietic and Kinetic minds. By himself the Voice forms his own caste of those excluded from the samurai. Soon after the Voice has reached his double, met him, and identified himself, the Voice juxtaposes his own unsuitability for utopia to the social instrumentality of the samurai.

In so identifying his life in the utopian terminology, he retains an identity characterized by an earthbound motivating energy or emotional life and a utopian name (or defense). The utopian ideal self behaves in the novel as the Voice's reassurance as well as the justification for presenting the larger utopian wish, and thus weakens the Voice's admitted rootedness and inextricability from the old earthly humiliations and frustrations. The ambivalence of the Voice's personality, as the figure who both invents and is a guest at the utopia he created, becomes the identity not only of himself but also of the entire utopia. The samurai—"the real body of the State" (277)—the group with whom utopia is ideally identified, along with the intellectual texture of the utopian world, constitute only the adaptive portion of the identity, the outward manifestation of a utopian personality that includes underneath the kind of emotional uncertainty and despair expressed by the Voice as he is about to meet his double.

In the work, however, the figure of the botanist, an earthly friend of the Voice who accompanies him on the galactic journey, also represents the uncertain portion of the identity. With respect to the Voice's conscious personality, the botanist appears to be something of an anomaly:

> It is strange, but this figure of the botanist will not keep in place. It sprang up between us, dear reader, as a passing illustrative invention. I do not know what put him into my head, and for the moment, it fell in with my humour for a space to foist the man's personality upon you as yours. . . . But here it is, indisputably with me in Utopia, and lapsing from our high speculative theme into halting but intimate confidences (25–26).

The botanist's capacity as a student of the stark Mother—his attachment to earth—behaves in his relationship with the Voice as the sign of the Voice's own uncertainty as to exactly what his relationship is with both the earthbound audience and the aspect of his own personality that the botanist represents. Psychologically, both of these relationships appear identical to the Voice, for the botanist's commitment to earth represents the audience's similar commitment, its rightfully assumed reluctance to accompany the Voice on his utopian trip. This imagined external reluctance on the parts of the botanist and audience is the Voice's *projection* of that part of his personality that is resisting the identification with the samurai ego-ideal. Just as the Voice characterizes his induced memories of his adolescence as "egotistical absorptions" (254), it is the botanist's being so "obsessed by himself and his own egotistical love" (69) and similar "incurably egotistical dissentients" (128) that stand in the way of utopian fulfillment: "Something is needed wide and deep enough to float the worst egotism away" (128). Where the samurai feels himself a man only after the second night with the stark Mother, the botanist, who "could waste our first evening in utopia upon a paltry egotistical love story" (124), prevents the Voice from reaching manhood—utopian identity—until he disposes of his initial egotistical love—the absorptions of his humiliating adolescence.

His relationship with the botanist is the preliminary stage in the formation of the Voice's identity. He wonders, as he is about to meet his utopian self, whether "he [the botanist] is really the human type or I" (232), where the determining parameter of humanity is "the profound difference in our imaginations" (231–232).

> I am not altogether without imagination, but what imagination I have has the most insistent disposition to square itself with every fact in the universe. It hypothesises very boldly, but on the other hand it will not gravely make believe. Now the botanist's imagination is always busy with the most impossible make-believe. That is the way with all children I know. But it seems to me one ought to pass out of it. It isn't as though the world was an untidy nursery; it is a place of splendours indescribable for all who will lift its veils. It may be he is essentially different from me, but I am much inclined to think *he* is simply more childish. Always it is make-believe (232).

The "act of imagination" by which both the botanist and the modern utopia came into being, however, was the Voice's, who describes his own act at the time as "one of these metaphysical operations that are so difficult to make credible" (133). The Voice's own activity, in his own words: "Make credible" is "always . . . make-believe" in this novel. Just as the childish imagination of the botanist is reproduced in the Voice's most important act in utopia—his creation of it—adult pleasures of lifting nature's veils, when partaken of by the best of utopian adulthood, the samurai, become acts of childhood, as when the samurai was "exploring the wilderness like a child." The Voice's conception of his own rationality, meanwhile, the impulse of his imagination "to square itself with every fact in the universe," is the intellectual defense that utopianism has traditionally invoked and operates on the "make-believe" principle that such reconciliation is possible at all. In all three, botanist, samurai, and Voice, the make-believe world of childhood generates their respective "fount of motives."

The persistence to the end of the novel of the botanist's "childish" outlook, however, finally grants him victory in his battle with the Voice. Their final argument is paradigmatic of the ambivalence in the work:

> "It's different here," I persist, "It's different here. The emotion you feel has no place in it. It's a scar from the earth—the sore scar of your past—"
>
> "And what are we all but scars? What is life but a scarring? It's *you* who don't understand! Of course we are covered with scars, we live to be scarred, we are scars! We are the scars of the past! These *dreams* these childish dreams—!"
>
> He does not need to finish the sentence, he waves an unteachable destructive arm.
>
> My utopia rocks about me. . . .
>
> We are in London, and clothed in the fashion of the town (357–8).

From his first appearance the botanist acted as an unconscious force to the Voice—"I do not know what put him into my head"—a notice of something intractable in the Voice's identity and the symbol of his inability to actually become the ideal he was able to imagine. In this final scene between the two, the habit of the botanist to "not keep in place" assumes the dramatic proportions it had all along assumed psychologically. The botanist has reached the Voice's status of reality in that he now proves capable of destroying what the Voice created. His ability to "rock" the utopia "about me," moreover, has the same affective power as the utopian double's ability to make the Voice's universe "sway" about him. The botanist has reached the same authority over the Voice that the latter consciously assigned to the samurai. Much as in the final reckoning, death, the child prevails in the samurai, the child botanist prevails over the Voice and kills him, so to speak, first by declaring the dreams "childish" and then by actually eliminating them from the face of the novel.

The botanist "does not need to finish the sentence" because with the habit of having "his hand [fly] out with a fluttering gesture of illustration" (2) that he has now overtaken from the Voice, he is able to "illustrate" the insubstantiality of the Voice's dreams. Back in London, however, when their relationship is ending in the midst of the "scars" of the real world, the Voice seeks revenge.

> For ten seconds or more I am furiously seeking in my mind for a word, for a term of abuse, for one compendious verbal missile that shall smash this man for ever. It has to express total inadequacy of imagination and will, spiritual anaemia, dull respectability, gross sentimentality, a cultivated pettiness of heart. . . .
>
> That word will not come. But no other word will do. Indeed the word does not exist. There is nothing with sufficient vituperative concentration for the moral and intellectual stupidity of educated people . . . (365).

Unlike the botanist, the Voice plainly *does* need to finish his sentence but remains unable to do it. Having created a whole book of words, the conclusion finds him unable to defend his book with the one additional word. He is reduced to infantile, temper-tantrum furiousness. Furthermore, the reference to "educated people'' once more recalls the slurs against the readers, who at the outset were identified with the botanist and who now resume this equivalence. The botanist-audience was originally "always" imagination, but now is afflicted with "total inadequacy of imagination," though obviously, the inadequacy portrayed in this passage is true only of the Voice. This Voice, with the defeat of his own act of imagination, has overtaken the character of the botanist; he cannot "smash this man for ever" because he has become the man that originally appeared "without the writer's intention" (372).[5] In this conclusion the lack of artistic intention and the lack of artistic identity for the work motivate one another.

Insofar as the Voice's impatience with the botanist derives from the latter's concern to regain his lost love, his "egotistical love story," his faith that the earthly flora are "mystically perfect and exemplary" (232), his absolute lack of "criticism about a horse or dog or woman!" (232), the "child's" world of the botanist ironically represents the heterosexual world of the novel, which suggests the Victorian tendency to think of the adult world as desexualized. In utopia, however, the reality is reversed: sexuality is the childish aspect, while the "adult world" (315) of the modern utopia is where the samurai "must sleep alone at least four nights in five" (297). The essential masculinity of the samurai consists of their transcendent reach to the stars, their discipline, their authority, and their chivalric personalities. The Voice's failure to identify with this ideal constitutes his failure to create a Victorian masculine identity, which would have overcome his grounding in the earth, humiliation, and impotence. In remaining dominated by his childish identity, his inner botanist, the Voice remains dominated by what he sees as a woman's world—a sexual world from which his Victorian wishes seek to remove him.

Much as the Potwell Inn offers the ultimate salvation for Mr. Polly's disgust with mercantile and sexual reality, the inns of the modern utopia utilize utopian technology to fulfill the Victorian wishes to deny sexuality. When the botanist, mulling over his love, mourns "the miserable waste of her" (57), he is immediately interrupted by the Voice's narration that "before us, through the tall pine stems, shine the lights of our Utopian inn" (57). The shift, as he puts it, "back to Utopia . . . speaking of travel" (59) represents the Voice's regressive translation of what in the botanist's mind is a familiar oedipal situation. The "waste" of his love is what he deems a marriage so unfortunate that "there are times when I could strangle him [the botanist's rival] with my hands" (59). What the Voice calls "egotism" is the exposed form of his own wish to reach the inns, which in utopia support and feed all travellers, returning them, so to speak, to their lost (maternal) love. In these inns, and especially in their "bedrooms," scientific virility and invention—a kind of Victorian fatherhood—joins the inn to resolve the Voice's anxiety. With few exceptions, the rewards of technology converge on the issue of sanitation—warm water bath, soap machine, towel dispenser. The room itself "has no corners to gather dirt" (104), and if some should appear, it is removed "with a few strokes of a mechanical sweeper" (104). In purifying the utopian bedroom, utopian technology has also purified the Voice's mind of the "memories of the foetid disorder of many an earthly bedroom after a night's use" (105). The word utopia "is enough to bring anyone out of bed, to the nearest window" (103) because bed is an especially "foetid" part of life. Like gold, which in utopia is all converted into less palpable "energy units," sexuality is also portrayed as an excremental product that is expunged by the advance of technology, by the "masculinity" of "sleeping alone four nights in five," and by the universal safety of the generous motherly inn.

"The heavy-eyed young Jewess" that is on earth a "draggled prostitute" (362) is seen through the window of the utopian inns as a "dusky little Jewess, red-lipped and amberclad," and instead of regarding "us with a momentary speculation," "passes me with unconscious disdain" (316). The earthly image of the Jewish prostitute unites the Voice's confusion of money, sex, and dirt in the old millenarian terms, the Jew as a social cancer. In utopia, the purified but disdainful Jew represents the amalgam of the Victorian wish for an omnipotent mother and the millenarian need to retain the image of the Jew as the castrating villain. This double role represents the double object of the utopian wish—to dispose of paternal authority and adult sexuality—an object achieved first by the samurai and then by conjugal regulations in the utopia at large. Although the samurai are ultimate in their authority, their chivalric character earmarked them as Victorian adolescent heroes—the "pure" men and the men emancipated from women and family. The responsibility for family—for the whole population—no longer belongs to the father but to the State, and this is "the only possible way" in which "things between the sexes" (188) can be equalized. Family functions—mainly the bearing and raising of children—are equated thereby to the ordinary professional functions of men. Such measures constitute the utopian response to the fact that women are "too commonly . . . an unwholesome stimulant" (202):

> The education, the mental disposition, of a . . . woman reeks of sex; her modesty, her decorum is not to ignore sex but to refine and put a point to it. . . . She outshines the peacock's excess above his mate (202).

The utopian double explains that under these sexual circumstances, women used wealth "to make underbred aggressions on other women," so that "as men emerged to civilisation, women seemed going back to savagery—to paint and feathers" (294). The utopian response is to a perceived ascendancy of sexuality and women in ordinary real life.

Two revealing drawings illustrating the text, and approved though not drawn by Wells, indicate the extent of the fantasy to which the Voice is responding. The drawing showing the woman outshining the peacock depicts a man carrying her, buckling under the strain, while she, excessively adorned, admires herself in a mirror. The drawing illustrating a woman's impulse to compromise in marriage because of her economic dependency, shows her on the aisle, tall and stately, her husband with satyr's ears and goat's feet, her mother tall and overweight, her father small and pusillanimous. Although the Voice claims that a woman's "incapacity for great stresses," her "liability to slight illnesses," her "weaker initiative, her inferior invention and resourcefulness, her relative incapacity for organisation" (187) all render her dependent on men, all three women in the drawings are inescapably stronger, prouder, and physically "sounder." The woman in the "peacock" drawing, moreover, is in physical ascendancy over the man; in both cases, the debilitation of the men seems the result not of feminine dependency but of a fantasy of feminine domination.

The masculine character of the novel's fantasy, then, insofar as it establishes a "Lesser Rule" for women, seeks to overcome the "child" in men that actually needs this condition of domination. This is the rationality behind the systematic subordination of women's rights—in spite of the apparent assertion of these rights—in utopia. In marriage, for example, "the one unavoidable condition will be the chastity of the wife" (194):

> Her infidelity being demonstrated, [the couple] must at once terminate the marriage and release both her husband and the State from any liability for the support of her illegitimate offspring. . . . A woman, therefore, who is divorced on this account will be divorced as a public offender. . . .
>
> A reciprocal restraint on the part of the husband is clearly of no importance whatever . . . (195).

The excessive sexuality previously attributed to women becomes "of no importance whatever" when overtaken by men, while the women's indulgences are deemed critical. Feminine sexuality is an intrusion into the masculine relationship with the State, with the utopia, and with his infantile fantasy, and is an emblem of uncontrolled sexuality in general. The Voice takes special advantage of his imaginative authority, acting as if he were himself the law controlling sexuality. If a couple fails to qualify to marry, that is, but

> conspire and add to the population of the State, we will, for the sake of humanity, take over the innocent victim of your passions, but we shall insist that you are under a debt to the State of a peculiarly urgent sort and one you will certainly pay. . . . It is a debt that has in the last resort your liberty as a security, and moreover, if this thing happens a second time, . . . we will take an absolutely effectual guarantee that neither you nor your partner offend again in this matter (184).

The Voice's appropriation of the pronoun "we" to indicate his personal authority in the service of part of the novel's fantasy—the wish to deny sexuality with pure adolescence—represents the Voice's confusion of identity. His wish to be the samurai is temporarily fulfilled, though he remains still the "Voice."

Just as the Voice's ambivalence of identity represents his struggle against his own sexuality and emotion—"Neither my Utopian double nor I love emotion sufficiently to cultivate it" (258)—the ambivalence of the work inhibits the emotional response of the audience. Because the Voice's personal identity is congruent with the novel's artistic identity, the response is challenged in the most basic sense—to compromise the suspension of disbelief, the artistic act of faith: what shall the reader believe? Is the world of the novel actually utopia, or is it just the Voice's imagination? Just as the Voice is caught between his being in utopia and his only imagining it, the reader must choose between being in a fictional world and only imagining being in a fictional world. The novel forces the reader to convey to the *reading experience* the imaginary conflict conjured up by the novel, thus:

UTOPIA
Samurai: utopian self

| | | | |
|---|---|---|---|
| conversation with own ideals | imagined conflict: Voice vs. samurai | victory over stars, planned world, control of sex, intellectual government | free dialogue with Father |

Voice: adolescent self

| | | | |
|---|---|---|---|
| conversation with own reality | reading experience: Voice vs. audience | irrational emotions, preoccupation with women, childish imagination, adolescent impotence | enforced dialogue with Mother |

Botanist: earthly self
AUDIENCE

In being addressed as "you" by the "we," the audience assumes the role of the Voice's lesser self, the botanist. Much as the botanist was interrupted by the Voice's drive to the inn, the narrative is interrupted by frequent admonitions to "figure" or imagine scenes that have already been conjured by the ongoing dialogue, as if the audience were a kind of inn-refuge from the threats of artistry. When, early in the work, the pair discovers a utopian gold coin, the Voice, before describing the coin, interjects, "You figure us on the high Gotthard road, heads together over the little disk that contrives to tell us so much about this strange world" (71). Likewise, when the pair is being identified, and the supervisor, realizing an apparent duplication, exclaims "but this is impossible!" (168), the scene is immediately abrogated by: "You figure us returning after a day or so of such Utopian experiences . . ." (168). In both cases, as soon as an incipient involvement is created in the utopian world, the Voice shifts from the upper world of utopia to the lower world of the audience. In this way, his uncertainty about the vision he has created is transferred to his relationship with the audience, who experiences it as an interruption of its suspension of disbelief.

The interruption of the audience's act of faith is the culmination of the sense of artistic uncertainty initially offered as the work's formal idiom. At the outset and at the conclusion, an italic metaVoice (his remarks are printed in italics) sets the stage by introducing the Voice and then clears the stage by announcing: "This is my all about utopia." He first introduces the "you must figure" habit by asking the reader to create the Voice: "You must figure the Owner of the Voice . . ." (2). Just as the Voice begins by announcing the "incurable effect of unreality" his work will have, the metaVoice initially rules out the customary formalisms of the lecture or the fiction, but he finally apologizes for "this conflicting form" (373). Wells's preface to the work, meanwhile, raised this same issue as a function of his own development as an artist. This was the work which, along with the two other earlier utopian essays, formed his "view-platform of the world" and was to be the jumping-off point of a subsequent career in fiction. Wells, the metaVoice, and the Voice are all intermediary figures in relation to this work: Wells in an intermediary career phase, the metaVoice as a quasi-real manager of the art to follow, the apologist for the conflicting form, and the Voice himself at the nexus of the conflicting form, shifting his own allegiance between the utopia and the audience. Insofar as these figures create the formal apparatus of the novel, they serve as the reader's first (would-be) reassurance that he or she can "trust" the work—or at least the experience of it. But if these reassurances are themselves ambivalent, the initial act of faith loses its authority and the coming reading experience promises only psychological danger.

Although Henry James seems to have sensed at least the literary danger of utopian Cheek, a danger suggested by his strategically denied judgments of invidiousness and disqualification, his response to the metaVoice seems genuinely appreciative, especially since the term "beauty" is not lavished on the rest of the work. "Your epilogue tag in italics," he wrote, "strikes me as of the highest, of an irresistable and touching beauty. Bravo, bravo, my dear Wells."[6] Why should such praise be forthcoming from James? The epilogue reads, in part,

this Utopia began upon a philosophy of fragmentation, and ends, confusedly, amidst a gross tumult of immediate realities, in dust and doubt, with, at the best, one individual's aspiration.
. . . This so-called Modern Utopia is a mere story of personal adventures among Utopian philosophies.

That greater scheme [of "the great State"] lies about the men and women I know, . . . about my talking couple, too great for their sustained comprehension. When one focuses upon these two that wide landscape becomes indistinct and distant, and when one regards that the real persons one knows grow vague and unreal. . . . In that incongruity between great and individual inheres the incompatibility I could not resolve, and which, therefore, I have had to present in this conflicting form. . . . For me, upon occasion, the little lures of the immediate life are seen small and vain, and the soul goes out to that mighty Being, to apprehend it and serve it and possess. But his is an illumination that passes as it comes, a rare transitory lucidity, leaving the soul's desire suddenly turned to presumption and hypocrisy upon the lips. One grasps at the Universe and attains—Bathos. The hungers, the jealousies, the prejudices and habits have us again . . . (373).[7]

Plainly, the speaker of this epilogue is the bathetic artist-hero in Wells, whose obverse comic identity James "drivels" at in the next paragraphs of his letter. For James this passage represents in Wells the dawning of that most precious commodity—awareness, a consciousness of the kind of unmistakable honesty that marks for James the artistic zenith of the work. James's citation of the "beauty" in the passage, the "irresistable and touching" beauty, suggests that he genuinely viewed it as an aesthetic triumph (cf. "touching" in the genesis of *The Golden Bowl),* which transcends the "Cheek" of the rest of the novel and which, along with *Kipps,* thus gives James the hope that Wells is ultimately convertable to his own kind of artistic identity. For James the formal circumscription ("epilogue tag") of the sense of failure and inadequacy expressed in the passage corresponds to his own defensive mode, just as Maggie's formal—social—triumph circumscribes the Prince's understanding that "everything is terrible . . . in the heart of man" in *The Golden Bowl.*

James's own need to indulge in such vicarious self-castigation and confessions of inadequacy, combined with the equally pressing need to "incorporate" Wells, permitted him to isolate the "beauty" of the passage from the "heroic Cheek" of the rest of the work. We who are not Transition readers of this novel, and who have more ordinary (nonutopian) motives with respect to Wells, may not hold this view. The confession represents to me the failure and the ambivalence present throughout the novel in the form of similar confessions and apologies by the Voice. The quest for the universe and the achievement of mere bathos operated not only in the polarity of samurai and botanist—i.e., in the final victory of the botanist—but also began in Wells's own life in the imagined quest for the stars and the simultaneous fear of incarceration on earth. This polarity is at the heart of the work's adolescent dilemma and produces both the confession of failure by the Voice and metaVoice and a corresponding response of "failure" on the part of this reader. Though we are not strictly conscious of it, the larger form of the work, the sequential structure of the 11 chapters, represents the failure, and thereby offers a fuller documentation for James's citation of the "beauty" in the epilogue. It suggests how the epilogue is the climax of failure.

The intellectual content of the work is a justification of its fantasy material. The first three chapters, "Topographical," "Concerning Freedoms," and "Utopian Economics," present a social machinery in which utopian individuals are free to roam all about the natural topography, "paying" only a minimum four hours per day of "work." Much as energy units replace coin as money, social structure is liquefied to the point where all have "the utmost freedom of going to and fro" (35) about the "entire planet," "no less" than which "will do" (11) for the modern utopia. The middle three chapters, "The Voice of Nature," "Failure in a Modern Utopia," and "Women in a Modern Utopia," articulate the position of utopian toleration for deviation, weakness, and emotion; discussions of bucolic and criminal man lead into the discussion of women. After an intellectual lull in a chapter called "A Few Utopian Impressions," the work faces its most important issues in "My Utopian Self," "The Samurai" (the longest chapter), and "Race in Utopia," where authority, religion, and ethnic solidarity are juxtaposed. The last chapter, which includes the italic epilogue, is called "The Bubble Bursts," where the botanist, the audience, and the Voice's sense of his own bathos gain the final ascendancy.

The emotional progress of the Voice, meanwhile, is a counterpoint to the train of intellectual development; where utopia exposes its authority, the Voice functions in dependency, and vice versa. In the first and third groups, the Voice is in subordinate relation to the ideological authority of utopia. He is, at first, on the "neck" and "shoulders" of Lucendro Pass, part of the commonality and formlessness of utopian freedom. As part of the economy, the Voice is employed at a toy factory, in a children's world, earning only minimum wage for a utopian citizen. The middle three chapters find the Voice in ascendancy over the utopian machinery—first over the tramp's dissenting Voice of Nature, the defender of "the face of our Mother" (108); next over the "failures, the invalids, idiots, madmen, and drunkards" (136); then over the samurai identification officer who is unenlightened as to the Voice's origins; and finally over the women, whose potential capacity for sexual offense the Voice himself threatens to punish. The utopian impressions the Voice receives while "trying not to feel too childish" (239) introduce the final four chapters, from whose utopian authority the Voice never recovers. The Voice's relationship to the intellectual issues, therefore, moves from "down" to "up" to "down," from childish dependency to secure and perhaps puguacious identity and back to dependency, ending at last in "bathos," where the "interplay of my vanities and wishes" joins with the final intellectual compromise: utopia ends "confusedly, amidst a gross tumult of immediate realities, in dust and doubt" (372). The bursting of the intellectual bubble finally releases the child—the botanist-Voice.

Each of the three groups, furthermore, works out a similar counterpoint of down-up-down. The first chapter of each group has at its center some idea of subordination. "Topographical" revolves around the physical bottom, the actual planet; "The Voice of Nature" is about the abject custodian of the planet, himself curling up like a "child;" and "My Utopian Self," in spite of its title, exposes the Voice's painful adolescent memories. The second chapters of each group portray a degree of initiative and authority. The Voice's free roaming of utopia, meanwhile, denigrates the botanist's "petty love story:" the freedom to control—and deny—love. The discussion of failure has the Voice succeeding in knowing his own identity, while the samurai are the peak of idealism. The final chapter in each group rounds out the motif with instances of sexual dependency. The conclusion of the "economics" discussion sees the Voice in the safety of the utopian inn triumphing over the "foetid disorder" of the bedroom. The discussion of women ends with the suggestion of "group marriage"—a fantasy of polygamy that relieves the embattled monogamous husbands in the two illustrations. And the discussion of race is finally documented by a visual survey by the Voice of the various races of *women* passing on the street corner on which he is standing. Where the concluding topic is always feminine, their two sides present the familiar adolescent polarity—the single nurturing inn against the multiple wives. The concluding activity of watching blends the infantile activity of *mere* watching with the adult masculine subject of attractive women, thereby holding the Voice in his adolescent way-station. All the world's women are his and not his at the same time.

The appearance of this tripartite movement in both horizontal and vertical directions only repeats the movements in Wells's life in both professional and personal senses. Professionally, he moved from the science-fiction/utopia phase, through a short span of mature fiction, to the extended attempts to realize utopia. He moved from the state of being professionally humored, to the phase of being taken somewhat seriously, to once again being humored, though now in the intellectual world. His personal life, likewise, moved from the limiting intimacy of marriage to his first cousin, through a short phase of genuine mutuality with Catherine Wells, and finally to the unstable adolescent search for the "right" woman in a series of *"passades."* The excessive monogamy of the early phase and the rakish promiscuity of the last correspond to the two extremes of adolescent ambivalence, and represent the projection onto domestic life of his struggle for identity.

For this reason, the "identity" of the work is formally ambivalent at the most detailed level of linguistic usage. In addition to the common linguistic habits of utopians (suggested in Chapter Five) overtaken by Wells, his own usage, considerably more prominent in the work, translates the traditional problem into his particular idiom of ambivalence. Take both the adult and juvenile senses of "play," for example. Play is more than an activity; it is the governing principle of social behavior. "To have free play for one's individuality is," the Voice observes, "in the modern view, the subjective triumph of existence" (32). "The final hope of the world" is in the "interplay of unique individualities'' (33). Domestically, ''we want to form households and societies . . . to give our individualities play in intercourse'' (38). Politically, statesmanship is regarded ''as a dramatic interplay of personalities'' (344). Internationally, ''the factor that leads the World State on from one phase of development to the next is the interplay of individualities'' (88). And phylogenetically, racial and hereditary classes will not develop because ''the intricate interplay of heredity is untraceable and incalculable'' (266). Because the business of play is what the Voice is engaged in in his toy factory and what assures his dependent status as a resident of the inn, once out of utopia, he returns to ''the interplay of my vanities and wishes,'' which represent the only ''individuality'' in the novel and the triumphant emotion in the figure of the ''childish'' botanist.

While the metaVoice confesses that the key to utopian conflict is the ''incongruity between great and individual spheres,'' the Voice is only able to attempt to resolve the incongruity insofar as he can differentiate himself from the botanist. After rejecting the botanist's wish for ''impeccable'' friends and his belief in a ''vegetable kingdom [that] is mystically perfect and exemplary'' (232), the Voice concludes: ''There is no perfection. . . . You cannot focus all good things together'' (233). Much as it is the botanist's imagination that the Voice actually overtakes in seeking an imagination that will ''square itself with every fact in the universe'' (232), and much as it is this same universe that he sought to reach in transcending the stars, the Voice, on his own, proclaims the perfection he confesses cannot be reached. The samurai are in ''perfect physical condition'' (159), and all other utopians have ''beautiful bodies, and a universally gracious carriage'' (172). Personal manner will be both ''universally tolerable'' (40) and ''universally diffused'' (70). Economically, there are ''perfected communications, perfected public services and economic organisations'' (173). Because there is ''easy access everywhere'' (45), the ''universal maximum of individual freedom'' (92) permits the ''happy holiday utopians'' (47) to travel ''everywhere'' on ''faultless roads'' (42). And intellectually, ''endless things will be understood perfectly and universally'' (40). Appearing in the work principally as a modifier—an adjective or adverb—the ''universe'' is the Voice's principle of transformation that retains its unreachable position by modifying objects of verbs of future tense. The final triumph of ''bathos'' had all along been implicit in the Voice's most basic and regular action—his use of language.

Yet a key proposal of the work calls for the emancipation from linguistic authority, for the deflation of the medium of the work's articulation. The early ridicule of the botanist as part of the philistine audience proceeds on the ground of their alleged demand for precise language:

You would make your ideal clear, a scientific language you demand, without ambiguity, as precise as mathematical formulae, and with every term in relations of exact logical consistency with every other. It will be a language with all the inflexions of verbs and nouns regular and all its construction inevitable, each word clearly distinguishable from every other word in sound as well as spelling (19).

To the more sensible Voice, on the other hand, language is "an animated system of imperfection" (22). An appended essay, "Scepticism of the Instrument," discussing the limitations of the mind imposed by ordinary language, emphasizes the fact that classificatory terms admit too fluid a content and lose their conceptualizing power when applied on an individual basis. This is the triumph of individuality over the fundamental intellectual instrument, language. Thinking of the botanist's wish, the Voice declares the "folly . . . of providing for the endless mysteries of the future a terminology and an idiom" (21). Nevertheless, the Voice's desire for universality remains to describe the utopian tongue. "The language of Utopia will no doubt be one and indivisible; all mankind will . . . be brought into the same phase, into a common resonance of thought" (22). It will be an amalgam of language coordinated by the "universal freedom of exchange and movement" (22). Any change taking place is "worldwide change; that is the quality of its universality" (22). When the "accursed bar of language" (17) is lifted, nations merge into each other and across the universe to utopia. But more, the removal of the barrier renders the Voice "free of the trammels of convincing story-telling" (17). It is utopian, in other words, to be free enough of language to be a writer that does not need to be convincing.

The ambivalence announced at the beginning reappears at the end to mark the work's and the utopia's formlessness. "Disregarding classes, cliques, sets, castes" (324), and the like, social forms, along with racial distinctions, are ironed out in the final vision. Earthly analogues to the utopian culmination are those which worked against these forms by minimizing linguistic differences.

> There was and there remains to this day, a profound disregard of local dialect and race in the Roman Catholic tradition, which has made that Church a persistently disintegrating influence in national life. Equally spacious and equally regardless of tongues and peoples is the great Arabic-speaking religion of Mohamet. Both Christendom and Islam are indeed on the secular sides imperfect realisations of a Utopian World State (326).

These two religious institutions, appearing as the only favorable proto-utopian models, restress in the last phases of the vision the implicit religious fantasy, and by association lead into the Voice's adolescent affirmation of utopian womanhood in his final view of racial integration. Where, at the beginning of the work, the lifting of language barriers and the consequent overthrow of the imperative to artful story-telling opened the door to union with the stark Mother, the "disregard" of linguistic variation at the end of the work allows the weakening of analogous social imperatives and permits the Voice his vision of religious merging with his universe.

Once this wish has been punctured—once "the bubble bursts"—and the botanist emerges victorious, the apocalyptic fantasy that has historically motivated the utopian fantasy emerges in Wells's novel:

> As my omnibus goes lumbering up Cockspur Street through the clatter rattle of cabs and carriages, there comes another fancy in my mind. . . . Could one but realise an apocalyptic image and suppose an angel, such as was given to each of the seven churches of Asia, given for a space to the service of the Greater Rule. I see him as a towering figure of flame and colour, standing between earth and sky, with a trumpet in his hands, over there above the Haymarket, against the October glow; and when he sounds, all the *samurai*, all who are *samurai* in Utopia, will know themselves and one another. . . .
>
> All of us who partake of the *samurai* would know ourselves and one another!
>
> For a moment I have a vision of this resurrection of the living, of a vague magnificent answer, of countless myriads at attention, of all that is fine in humanity at attention, round the compass of the earth.
>
> Then that philosophy of individual uniqueness resumes its sway over my thought, and my dream of a world's awakening fades (368–369).

In an unfortunate sense, the progress of the work had led to the necessity for just such a conclusion, that is, to the necessity to *expose* this fantasy; some such feeling had been part of every phase of the novel. Here, control is abandoned; what was previously partially imagined or "fictionalized" is now offered in the form of a wish. The usual combination of a future tense and imperative "suppose" or "figure" gives way to the subjunctive—"Could one but realise. . . ." The "philosophy" of uniqueness or individuality, in resuming its own "sway," causes the same destruction of identity as did the botanist's wave of his arm that caused utopia to "rock about me" and as did the presence of the samurai double which caused the Voice's own "universe" to "sway." The would-be power of the "apocalyptic image" is easily defeated by the "childish" world of "interplay." The allusion to the Asian churches and the vision of their mysterious power are benevolent inversions of the *fin de siècle* fear of invasion by some "yellow menace" that would overrun the land and cause a true apocalypse. Caught "between the earth and sky," between the two poles of his personality, the military metaphor is revived, and resolution is sought through merging with "all humanity"—"all of us would know ourselves"—all would stand at attention, under the "big-brother" leadership of the "towering figure" and enclose or incorporate "the compass of the earth."

The less personal component of James's response to this work, the judgment of "beauty" in the metaVoice's final lamentation, locates the common ground of identity between James and Wells in the adolescent phase of possibility without power; the aspiration to the universe and rootedness in bathos: the activation of the deepest infantile energies and the awareness of their vanity. James was touched because he must have been like Wells in having made the discovery about himself. But he grew beyond Wells because his world of artistic awareness was able to reach the universal proportions that Wells sought to reach in reality. He was able to convert reality into his museum of consciousness and thus create an adult identity from the same emotional constellation, and perhaps the same fantasy, that paralyzed Wells in adolescence.

**8**

# *The Golden Bowl:* **The Artistic Translation of the Utopian Fantasy**

Perhaps one of the most convincing indicators of the adult or nonutopian cast of James's "great good place" is that it took him a lifetime to reach it; he was consciously displeased when he faced the content of "The Great Good Place," but he deemed *The Golden Bowl* of "rarest perfection." The world of the imagination was of course with him from his beginnings as a writer, but its artistic power, organized by the idea of "point of view" and by his intuitive sense of the primacy of subjective life, passed through an arduous development and was accorded its status of perfection only after many struggles—personal and professional. The linkage of his sense of self with his sense of artistic perfection represented a real achievement, inwardly perceived and critically recognized.

In an important sense, critical appreciation of the work lay in the rearticulation of the moral victory it dramatized. There is a general satisfaction with the work's balance and resolution of moral and social power, a sense of both reality and rightness in Maggie's achievement. In this way, the work of the novel wins serious attention in our culture. Noting the work's important position in James's career, for example, Stephen Spender writes: "The question James has not yet answered is whether it is possible in the modern world to choose to live: and Maggie triumphantly answers it for him."[1] Similarly, Oscar Cargill noted that "no novelist produces so clear a moral tone with so little suspicion of didacticism."[2] Frequently, the ethical victory is translated directly into the Christian terms of Western ethics. Caroline Gordon sees the motivating force of the novel as "caritas, Christian charity,"[3] and Frederick Crews notes the "Christlike size of Maggie's love," who herself "reminds us of Christ."[4] Like Christ, Maggie confronted Evil and emerged victorious. In these most common, most traditional terms, Maggie's actions represents triumph for both art and life.

This consensus, in that it accepts Maggie's own perception of her victory and in that it takes the ethical cast of this perception as essential, however, underestimates the governing principle of her half of the novel—its near-total setting in Maggie's point of view. Crews did write that "hard facts, the real basis for the drama, never rise to the surface at all,"[5] yet still maintains the certainty of Maggie's victory. It is difficult to see how such certainty is tenable with so few facts, unless the facts themselves are of a different kind than the usual ones found in novels. The paucity of facts, alongside the "fact" of Maggie's victory, is therefore reconcilable only if the victory is viewed as a total function of Maggie's perspective. In other words, *there is no way of determining "objective reality" in this novel* because nearly all of what we would ordinarily call "facts" are either reported or imagined by Maggie. It is unimportant in the second half of the novel what "really" happens; it is only important what Maggie either believes or *says* she "knows." This "knowledge" is what creates both her own literary personality and the emotional atmosphere of the second half of the novel. This half represents Maggie's response to the first half of the novel, which *is* credibly viewed as "objective" in the ordinary sense. It is noteworthy in this connection that only the material in Book First appeared in James's early notes for the work, so that the creation of Maggie's victory and the achievement of James's own coincide. Maggie's victory, insofar as it retains its Christian flavor, can also be understood as *the victory of the Christian fantasy whose totality assumes the form of subjective consciousness.* This new consciousness is the artistic form of utopia.

The extent to which Maggie's consciousness directs social and ethical functioning is the extent to which it is *introjecting* the adverse social situation it confronts, and to which it *renounces* that situation's external presence. Maggie's consciousness creates the illusion of social interplay while actually enlarging its subjective domain with its many purely personal fantasies about the relationships she is reacting to. The merging of consciousness with the social relationships is the novel's means of offsetting the developments in Maggie's fantasy-life, a means observable in the various metaphors and other subtleties of language use. The overall form of the novel, moreover, coincides with this pattern of defense and fantasy, in that Book First is objective and Book Second subjective. Maggie's half of the novel represents a renunciation of the "evil" she has experienced, of the presence of her father, and the conquest, correspondingly, of the "evil" pair, Charlotte and the Prince, through her introjection of them and through the occupation, in her imagination, of her father's museum. The introjected form of this museum is her own consciousness.

Accordingly, the Galerie d'Apollon, which James described as "the world . . . raised to the richest and noblest expression,"[6] finds an analogue in Adam's proposed museum in American City, which was "positively civilisation condensed, concrete, consummate," emanating the "highest knowledge."[7] While Maggie, in Book First, is herself viewed as an object in Adam's collection, the opening pages of Book Second suggest a new role for her. She now "walks round and round," a "strange, tall, tower of ivory," but in which as yet "no door appeared to give access" (289). This structure represents her perception of the status of the relationships in Book First, "as she liked to put it, her having been able to marry without breaking . . . with her past" (290). Some time later she enters the edifice; she passes "along the corridor of her life," where, every now and then, "by a mental act" she "pushed a door open" (297) to deposit a new element of intelligence. As she is thus ruminating, "quite a different door had opened and her husband was there" (297), arriving into her parlor from his adulterous afternoon at Matcham to confront Maggie's yet unarticulated suspicion. Nearing her climactic discovery, it is "her time at the Museum" (400) that inspires her trip to Bloomsbury, where she ultimately comes upon the golden bowl. With the shattering of the bowl, again in her parlor, "the door of the room had been opened by the Prince" (416), and Maggie reveals to him her new knowledge. Finally, in the closing scene of the novel, as Adam is about to depart for America, he surveys his legacy to Maggie, in which, in addition to all the "good things" of art, is found "the kind of human furniture required, aesthetically, by such a scene" (542), Charlotte and the Prince. The collection in her "museum" is now complete. Much as James's "mental act" of dreaming allowed him to push open the door and take command of the Galerie d'Apollon, Maggie's own mental acts, her images of the tower and the pagoda, her trip to the museum, push open the door to her private museum—an act externalized in the Prince's door-openings—where she confronts the Prince over the broken bowl, "knowing everything" (421). Maggie's enlarged edifice of knowledge in Book Second is the introjected form of Adam's museum of Book First.

The image of the boat, perhaps less prominent in James's vocabulary, underscores the essential isolation of Maggie's consciousness. In the novel's opening conversation, after Maggie jokingly includes the Prince in her father's collection, the Prince jokes back by wondering if he is "so big that I have to be buried" in the "tomb" (9) of American City. As if apprehending the serious content of the joke, the Prince seriously asks Maggie if she has faith in his integrity, but she jokingly returns that her faith is divided "into water-tight compartments. We must manage not to sink" (9). The Prince apparently realizes the "compartment" he is already in: "He had noticed it before: it was the English, the American sign that duplicity like 'love' had to be joked about. It couldn't be 'gone into' " (9). Having thus trapped or entombed the Prince, Maggie completes the figure:

> Water tight—the biggest compartment of all? Why it's the best cabin and the main deck and the engine-room and the steward's pantry! It's the ship itself—it's the whole line. It's the captain's table and all one's luggage—one's reading for the trip (10).

Working in the manifest ethical sense, Maggie's "good faith" here reaches its infinite Christian proportions—the entire trip through married life, including the engine and the food. Underneath the joke, though, is the Prince's stifled seriousness, and like her consciousness in Book Second, Maggie's metaphorical joking is as impervious as it is ubiquitous.

As the social situation first joked about is crystallized later in Book First, the Prince finally observes to Fanny that he and Charlotte are "in the same boat" (188), but this time without Maggie, and without the joke it emerges as "Mr. Verver's boat," which keeps them "pecuniarily afloat": "but for Mr. Verver's boat, I should have been by this time . . . down, down, down" (188). In Book First, Adam's boat, like his museum, is the informing entity of the social situation; both the enclosing vessel and the sustaining body of fluid circumscribe the two non-Ververs. The completion of Maggie's "idea" in Book Second occurs when Adam announces that he is "shipping out" to American City and the museum. But by now all action has been transferred to Maggie's consciousness as the novel returns to Maggie's opening figure of the "tomb"-museum with all the "good things" and "human furniture."

With both the Prince and Adam effectively out of the dramatic picture, it becomes clear how, as Austin Warren has already observed, "the violent relation is between two women,"[8] and how this relation takes the center of the stage of Maggie's museum-consciousness, much as the Galerie was the scene of James's triumph over his own archrival. Viewing Charlotte at a bridge game, Maggie sees the "evil" she represents as having met her (Maggie) "like some bad-faced stranger in one of the thick-carpeted corridors of a house of quiet on a Sunday afternoon" (455). Subsequently, at Fawns, she exchanges glances with her father "from end to end of the great gallery . . . as if, in one of the halls of a museum" (490), where she then brings Adam into the service of her fantasy by imagining him telling her: "I lead her now by the neck, I lead her to her doom, and she doesn't know so much as what it is" (492). In the final confrontation with Charlotte, the museum is completely introjected as she envisions her departing "down the long vista" (513). At last alone with the Prince in the room where he and Charlotte had just been viewed as "human furniture," she suggests to him that Charlotte is "dying for us" (532). The subordination of the Prince to Maggie's vision of the dying Charlotte is signalled by his repeated qualifying remark, "as you say," so that he is now brought fully into Maggie's fantasy through her linguistic idiom.

Where the image of death defines the violence of Maggie's feelings about Charlotte, the ground of her imagined victory is the denial of Charlotte's subjective capacities. She imagines Charlotte "having gropingly to go on, always not knowing and not knowing" (433); she creates the image of Charlotte in a "suspended cage . . . of eternal unrest" (449), in a "deluded condition" of "baffled consciousness" (449). And she asserts to Fanny, without any documentation, that Charlotte will not tell Adam of her (Maggie's) discovery because she is held "by her ignorance" (524). Knowledge, or consciousness, is Maggie's only weapon in the battle, for in comparing herself to Charlotte as a social—really, sexual—being, the latter is the unqualified winner. While awaiting, in deep uncertainty, the Prince's return from his afternoon with Charlotte at Matcham, she transfers her uncertainty to her clothing: "She had ever been, in respect to her clothes, rather timorous and uncertain; for the last year, above all, she had lived in the light of Charlotte's possible and rather inscrutable judgement of them" (296). The image is soon expanded, however, into remarkable dimensions. Charlotte's clothes were "simply the most charming and interesting that any woman ever put on." But more, Charlotte soon becomes a woman of "omnipotence" and "genius," "great in life," and radiating "so perfect a critical vision" (296). She further imagines Charlotte as having "given her up as hopeless" and wonders if she had not "assented in secret despair, perhaps even in secret irritation, to her being ridiculous" (297). On the battleground of clothing and social bearing, Maggie conceives of herself as the ridiculous facing the sublime. But this outer sphere, this world of Book First, is the antithesis, renounced and introjected, through which Maggie defines her triumphant thesis. Once introjected, Charlotte's attributes are for naught; on the battleground of "knowledge," Charlotte is the unequivocal loser, for she is "always not knowing" where Maggie is "knowing everything." When introjected, omnipotence becomes omniscience, and this is what secures Maggie's victory. In the museum of consciousness, the "bad-faced stranger" is "led to her doom."

In a general sense—dramatic, social, and sexual—the male figures in Maggie's life are subordinate, so that all action is initiated by either her, Fanny, or Charlotte. This subordination isolates the battle between Maggie and Charlotte. Charlotte, in fact, is the prime initiator of social action, as in her opening appearance, when she sets the stage for the subsequent battle with Maggie. Her first words on arriving for the wedding—"You see you're not rid of me. How is dear Maggie?" (33)—prefigure the emergence of the old love affair but also relate this affair to its new factor, Maggie. Characteristically, the Prince sees her approach in an ambivalent key, first seeing in her the "sylvan head of a huntress," but when she approaches him she takes on "his notion . . . of a muse" (33). This ambivalence, perhaps earlier crystallized by Maggie's consigning him to the tomb, renders him a mere excuse for the main emotional confrontations, as he subsequently retains no options either to initiate or resist. It is Charlotte who requests the hour "alone" (65) with the Prince and who then offers him the gift of the bowl ostensibly intended for Maggie. During the rendezvous at Matcham, a sense of their own harmony overtakes the Prince and Charlotte: "they were conscious of the same necessity at the same moment," but the crucial factor was that "it was she, as a general thing, who most clearly saw her way to it" (253). Thus, when the Prince calls on her, not only is she dressed and prepared, but has also arranged for meals and transportation to

Gloucester and back to London. She tossed him a flower, and he placed "it in his button hole" (254). She appeared to him a Pearl, and "its value grew . . . in his hand" (254). Hers is the sexual initiative. Clearly it was so when she arrived that important day unheralded at the Prince's home and approached him whence "everything broke up, broke down, gave way, melted and mingled" (221).

Sexuality between the Prince and Maggie, meanwhile, is (expectedly) rare in the novel, but it depends in any case on Maggie's stipulations. The Principino arrives on the scene neither as the Prince's nor Maggie's son, but as the "grandson" of Adam, and is immediately ranked as another of his "precious small pieces" (103). Like the Prince, that is, his son is a collected item. Of the three occasions where a sexual encounter is conceivably imminent, all are controlled by Maggie's wishes, and coincidentally or not, never materialize. The first is when the Prince arrives from Matcham. Maggie has an elaborate fantasy of how she might declare her love to him, how she is as much in love with him now "as the first hour" (300), but this declaration is "what *didn't* ring out" (300). Instead she is held, silently, at his breast, "in hesitation" (300); she offers to help him dress but is refused because of the later dinner hour, though her "agitated overture" (308) is, "after all, unmistakably met." Subsequently, as Maggie gains more "knowledge," she also gains more control and a decisive veto power on lovemaking, a power which is exercised to the last.

On the last two occasions, her love is available to the Prince only with the stipulation of some verbal commitment on his part. Her conscious plan becomes one to send the Prince away with her father while she attends to Charlotte. In confronting the Prince with her plan, he responds in his own idiom, "her husband's silence," and a gathering embrace, which evokes in Maggie the wish-fantasy that he would ask *her* to "come away with me, somewhere—*you*" (330), which in turn would allow her to accede to his overtures. Whether by Maggie's own early circumscription of his possibilities for action, or by his own usual idiom, or probably both, the Prince sticks to his own silent embrace and to Maggie's verbalized plan. Maggie does not respond, therefore, and instead "slipped from him during their drive" (335). The Prince is thus kept at bay as Maggie's own idiom of action takes a decisive step from an "agitated" physical initiative to a controlled denial of his initiative. The underlying wish in Maggie for the Prince to overture in *her* idiom, to ask to take her away, is revealed in the final chapter when she asks the Prince the most important question in her whole campaign: "Am I to take from you that you accept and recognize my knowledge" (535)? An affirmative answer by the Prince would fulfill her most basic wish, that her knowledge be *recognized*. The Prince, however, responds in his usual silence, in a delayed request to "wait" (535), and a physical approach which once more evokes her "weakness, her desire" (537) and the possibility of accession. But now in the final triumph, "the right word came"

(537), as he approaches near enough for her to "touch him, taste him, smell him, kiss him, hold him" (537). The word is his own "wait," which she twice repeats. She had for the last time in the novel "saved herself" (537). She remains only with the fantasy of public recognition, and without its coordinate sexuality. Sexuality is thereby related to knowledge, where the latter is Maggie's form of sexuality. Like knowledge, sexuality is confined only to her fantasy, with the possible exception of the vaguely verbalized "agitated overture." Love, or verbal expressions of it, is precisely what didn't ring out in Maggie, though she makes the identical demand for such verbalizations from the Prince. Maggie's love, which can hardly be deemed "Christlike" in this connection—though it easily appears so—is like her conquest of Charlotte, a function only of her subjectivity.

Mistaken attention to the marital issues of the novel as its center, deriving from the questionable notion that Maggie's love is socially directed, is typified by Joseph Ward's observation that "the Golden Bowl stands for Maggie's marriage,"[9] with the crack representing the adulterous defect. There are, it seems to me, not enough grounds for this assertion. Maggie tells Fanny that "I want a happiness without a hole in it . . . the golden bowl—as it *was* to have been. . . . The bowl with all the happiness in it. The bowl without the crack" (440). Rather than a wish for a perfect marriage, which Maggie never explicitly seeks, the bowl of happiness is more convincingly understood as the wish for a perfect *consciousness,* the knowledge within which is frequently sought. Maggie explains to Fanny just before the above metaphorical declaration that "I put him in possession of the difference . . . made about me by the fact that I hadn't been. I'm changed for him. . . . It became a question then of his really taking in the change" (440). This description of her actual desire—her wish that the Prince recognize her knowledge—refers back to the climactic scene where Maggie is confronting the Prince over the broken pieces of the golden bowl. Just before Maggie reveals her knowledge to the Prince, she lifts the two halves of the bowl and momentarily anneals them with her hands "before her husband's eyes" (419). This act is an externalized, deverbalized form of the silent demand Maggie, in fantasy, makes of the Prince moments later to "See, see that *I* see" (420). As if in answer to this passionate question, the Prince's last words to Maggie in the novel are, "See? I see nothing but *you*" (548), where Maggie's italicized "I" and the Prince's italicized "you" refer to the same person. Rather than a condition of mutuality, as is usually *inferred* to be represented by the bowl, the sum of Maggie's silent wishes—her pantomime and her verbalized wishes to Fanny—sketches out a performance which demands from the Prince only the recognition of her strength—a sense in him of her ascendancy in the matter. The Prince's further requests for information about anyone else's knowledge of her discovery evoke Maggie's almost imperious taunt, "find out for yourself," a demand twice made. As with the Prince's sexual overtures, his requests for any kind of "knowledge" are forced to accede to Maggie's authority. The Prince is brought under the aegis of Maggie's consciousness and not, as is often claimed, of her marriage.

The critical response to the bowl as a symbol of marriage is an important testimony to its successful artistic function as a machinery for disguising Maggie's growth toward a monolithic subjectivity. The bowl represents the keystone of the work's formal framework. Through Fanny Assingham, the connection between the bowl and the larger framework is made at the climax of the novel. As the novel's *"ficelle,"* Fanny objectifies James's link with the work, and serves as a kind of alter ego for Maggie in her "objective" social world of Book First. In a sense, Fanny precipitates the whole drama by arranging the marriage of Maggie and the Prince to begin with. Although very little is told about Fanny's personal life, two apparent facts about it identify her with Maggie. First, with regard to Fanny's motivation in arranging the marriage, her husband suggests:

> What happened . . . was that you fell violently in love with the Prince yourself, and that as you couldn't get *me* out of the way you had to take some roundabout course. *You* couldn't marry him, any more than Charlotte could—that is not to yourself. But you could to somebody else—it was always the Prince, it was always marriage. You could to your little friend, to whom there were no objections (57).

Fanny assents to this "exposure of the spring of her conduct" by reaffirming that "it *is* always the Prince, and it *is* always . . . marriage" (57). More importantly, perhaps, this wish of Fanny's derives from her "precious power of thinking whatever you do want" (57). Early in the novel, therefore, Fanny is presented, obliquely, as operating at the behest of what is later to become Maggie's defining personal characteristic, her autocratic consciousness, which, in turn, legislates the immovable terms of the relationship with the Prince— "always marriage." Fanny initiates in the objective social world what Maggie rounds out in triumphant subjectivity.

Toward the end of Book First, when the two adulterous marriages are fully launched, and new action for Maggie is dictated, a similar identification occurs. "You remember," Fanny remarks to her husband, "how I continued, *tout bêtement,* to adore my mother, . . . for years after I had begun to adore you. Well, Maggie . . . is in the same situation as I was" (281). Here, then, as with the causal factors in Maggie's marriage, Fanny identifies with the etiology of the marriage's weakness, the continued attachment to the parent. Furthermore, in imagining Maggie's course of action under the circumstances, she sees her as "an old woman who has taken to 'painting' and who had to lay it on thicker, to carry it off with greater audacity, with a greater impudence even, the older she grows" (281). In one sense, Fanny transforms Maggie into a woman of experience like, perhaps, herself; in a more definitive sense, the paint, and just afterwards, the ''rouge'' she sees Maggie using, casts her as a pathetic, transparent seductress, whose maneuvering is epitomized in ''impudent'' and ''audacious'' sexual aggression, underscoring a *false* sense of self-importance. This new prognosis of Fanny's enlarges her own original audacity in her alleged wish to get the Prince for herself. Fanny's identification with Maggie, in any case, acts as a distracting foil that helps to conceal the aggressive energy, implicit but pervasive, in the novel's heroine.

Fanny, in a more denotative sense, defines Maggie's social and moral destiny. At first she pronounces Maggie ''not born to know evil'' (54) but by the end of Book First, in the same conversation about the ''paint,'' she concludes that Maggie's ''sense will have to open . . . to what's called 'Evil' '' (273). By the middle of Book Second, the prophecy comes true when Maggie sees ''evil seated . . . where she had only dreamed of good'' (455). Furthermore, Fanny's equation—''What is morality but high intelligence'' (62)—early in the novel lends Maggie's subsequent dominating and passionate search for ''intelligence'' its face of justice and ethical integrity. Yet this face, with its task of dealing with evil itself, and with its technique of doing so through intelligence, is the crux of the characteristic utopian strategy from its very beginnings with More. The fact of the novel's arthood, however, substitutes, for utopia's move toward reality, the enlargement of consciousness, and in this way *consciousness achieves its utopian range*. The normally externally directed utopian move is introjected by the artwork into Maggie's mind, though it is externally disguised by the more or less technical existence of Fanny Assingham, her moral pronouncements and social functions.

While Fanny's dashing of the golden bowl helps to identify her with Maggie, this dashing is the climax of Maggie's subjective development because it destroys the symbol, though it fulfills the actuality, of her wish for a perfect consciousness. At this point, Fanny's externalizing function reaches its most extreme form. After Maggie asserts that the bowl gave her conclusive proof of the adultery of the Prince and Charlotte, Fanny raises the bowl saying, ''if it's because of this [bowl],'' and dashes ''it boldly to the ground'' (416) in a final, outward attempt to destroy the intelligence it brought—but also to destroy the possibility of communicating this intelligence to the Prince and to lock it in Maggie's consciousness. As the two women note the shattered bowl on the ground, Fanny ''flushed with the force of her effort'' and Maggie ''flushed with the wonder at the sight,'' the action is frozen by the ''high reflection'' of each other. Behind these flushes of both identification and knowledge, however, lies a more determining and more damaging emotion, as Fanny experiences the ''thrill of seeing it, with the violence of the crash, lie shattered'' (416). Although, at this instant, the violence is forthcoming from Fanny, as is the thrill in its performance, this act remains an externalized form of what had hitherto been latent in Maggie, what had been brewing all along. A few minutes later, after the Prince has entered the scene, Maggie experiences a "thrill at seeing the Prince straitened and tied" as she contemplates the "ravage of suspense and embarrassment, produced, and produced, by my doing, in your personal serenity, your incomparable superiority" (420). By itself, in fact, the "thrill of seeing" is the apex of Maggie's subjective accomplishment, for certainly this thrill is at the crux of her passionate request to the Prince to "see that *I* see." The thrill extends its range to Charlotte as well, for, as Charlotte approaches her on the bridge-room terrace in the first of their two important confrontations, her feelings are "all a thrill" (455), and they seem as violent—and as remote—as a "wild eastern caravan," a "natural joy to mingle with" (455). Yet these thrilling feelings occur on the occasion when she had just observed Charlotte as "evil seated where she had only dreamed of good" and when Charlotte appears as the "bad-faced stranger" approaching her in the "house of quiet." All of these thrills must be of the same emotional cloth as the "thrilling use" to which James's dream put the Galerie d'Apollon, the use of conquest, power, and victorious exultation. The breaking of the bowl projects all of the apocalyptic violence of Maggie's boiling, though essentially unconscious, aggressive energies onto Fanny in this last and most distinct act of identification, and thereafter, the violence emerges as a function of Maggie's subjectivity.

The distancing provided by Fanny as an alter ego for Maggie's not-so-latent violent feelings finds an important correlative in Maggie's own subjectivity—her abiding sense of "strangeness" associated with the turbulence in her life. This feeling is most clearly articulated in the fact that Charlotte is metaphorically converted into a "stranger." In a realistic sense, the feelings Maggie experiences might be conceived as being strange in the sense of foreign, of not having had them before; in a more important sense, strangeness represents Maggie's refusal to recognize the violence for what it is. Her desire to accede to the Prince's sexual advances, for example, seems "strange, inexpressably strange." She feels unable to cope with these feelings and imagines them forcing her to "give up everything forever" (330). The bowl, she explains to Fanny, "is strangely—too strangely, almost . . . the proof" (404), much as she had invited Fanny over to begin with by informing her that "something very strange has happened" (399). Almost everything connected with her discovery and its implications for what she must do appears either strange or odd or funny, while other feelings, as if independent of this enigmatic one, force upon her thrilling feelings of power.

Her sense of detachment from her violent feelings emerges when, just as she is about to pick up the pieces of the bowl before the Prince's eyes, she experiences the strangeness of her desire to spare him, a strangeness that had already fifty times, brushed her, in the depth of her trouble, as with the wild wing of some bird of the air who might blindly have swooped for an instant into the shaft of a well, darkening there by his momentary flutter the far-off round of the sky (421).

Maggie, as was suggested in the opening conversation with the Prince, conceives of herself as a woman of almost infinite magnanimity and "good faith" living in a universe whose "round sky" holds only mercy, only the "desire to spare." At this moment, however, her desire, her previous and prevailing self-concept, appears to her as a strange bird clouding her ethical horizon. Having reached full knowledge, her ethical charitable impulses appear strange, for knowledge is her weapon that just seconds later will cause the "ravage of suspense and embarrassment" on her "incomparable" husband. At this moment, therefore, Maggie's unarticulated sense of violence causes the unaccountable adulteration of her conceived magnanimity. Her way of expressing this new feeling is to create a metaphor of a bird with a "wild wing" that passes over the shaft of her good will "fifty times." This metaphor represents her own art, as well as the novel's, for it spares *her* the painful task of recognizing the violent source from which her deceptive sense of her own kindness grows. Her kindness is "strange" because it is not really kind.

The bowl leads further into a "well" of apocalyptic depths, since its discovery and destruction leads in her life to "the end to such a history" (521). In the dramatic terms of the novel, this is the *"whole* history of the relation" (519) between Charlotte and the Prince that Maggie succeeded in penetrating—the "evil" in her life that she overcame. Before reaching the apocalyptic sphere, however, history passes through two other cultural transformations, through the Prince and through Adam, and the quasi-mythic processes of civilization they represent. The Prince represents the quintessential product of modern Western civilization, "somehow full of his race" (10) yet culturally including the "old golden Rome," from which the discoverer of the New World was descended, the Prince's namesake, and which was the scene of the "accepting . . . of Amerigo's proposal of marriage" (294). On one hand the Prince's personal past includes the "history, the doings, the marriages, the crimes, the follies, the boundless *betises* of other people" (5). On the other it includes the ecclesiastical storms of "the wicked Pope, the monster most of all" (6), all of which are enshrined in the lasting cultural record—"so many of the volumes in your family library" (6). The Prince's consciousness of this history brings him into the novel "steeped as in some chemical bath. . . . He knew his antenatal history . . . and it was a thing to keep causes well before him" (10). In this historical sense, the Prince is already afloat, his new situation represented by Maggie's awe before this sea "sweetened the waters in which he now floated" as if "poured from a gold-topped phial for making one's bath aromatic" (6). The historical "bath," joined with the sense of "antenatal" development, creates the image of the pre-Maggie Prince as immersed in the historical amniotic fluid that witnesses both phylogenetic and ontogenetic development.

The Prince's transformation, under Maggie's aegis, into an "old gold coin," like the sweetening of his historical waters with Maggie's "gold-topped" bath oil, represents a necessary culmination of his history:

> What was it but history, and of their kind very much, to have the assurance of the enjoyment of more money than the palace builder himself could have dreamed of? This was the element that bore him up and into which Maggie scattered, on occasion, her exquisite colouring drops. They were of the colour of . . . what but the extraordinary American good faith? They were the colour of her innocence, and yet at the same time of her imagination, with which their relation, his and these people's, was all suffused (6).

Maggie's imagination and good faith, linked in her image of the "whole line" of her good faith in the Prince, the ship carrying them as a married couple in society, here "bore him up." Her imagination and good faith are widened, through her coloring capacity, into a semiartistic agent that is giving a new life to the Prince. Maggie's giving birth to him from the sea of his history has the effect of killing him through the paralyzing function of art. This simultaneous act of artistic creation and murder is a principal source of James's—and Maggie's—actions. Saving the Prince from his history is the culmination of the history, but by thus ending it, it is killed in favor of the establishment of the American Princess. Here coloring, innocence, imagination, good faith are instrumentally mobilized by her—and her father's—American-made wealth, which, in bailing the Prince out, incarcerates him in the wealth of Maggie's omniscient "point of view."

The Prince early in the novel conceives of a "desire for some new history that should, so far as possible, contradict, and even if need be flatly dishonour the old. . . . He perfectly recognized . . . that the material for the making had to be Mr. Verver's millions. There was nothing else for him on earth to make it with" (10). But in keeping himself "pecuniarily afloat" (188) in Adam's sea and ship, the Prince moves to a prehistoric precivilized realm—Adam's mythic garden at Fawns. In this garden, Maggie—in Book First—is in a parental role alongside her father. When the Principino was born, "what was clear" was Maggie and Adam's

> simply knowing they wanted for the time to be together—at any cost, as it were; and their necessity worked on them as to bear them out of the house . . . to wander, unseen, unfollowed, along a covered walk in the "old" garden, . . . old with an antiquity of formal things. . . . They went out a door in the wall . . . they gradually passed to where some of the grandest trees spaciously clustered and where they would find one of the quietest places. A bench had been placed long ago, beneath a great oak that helped to crown a mild eminence. They knew the bench; it was "sequestered"—they had praised it for that together, before, and liked the word . . . (111–112).

With the Principino having already been introduced into the novel as Adam's grandson rather than the Prince's son, a new closeness between father and "daughter" ensues. Passing out of the door into an "antiquity," they arrive at the "sequestered" grove on the "mild eminence" of which is the "great oak." (It might be recalled that the "noble eminence of our hill" in "The Great Good Place" was also the "bosom" at which Dane and the Brother found their most satisfying rest.) The familiarity which this grove holds for both of them, a closeness identified by their mutual affection for the word "sequestered," is expressed in Maggie's most important idiom: "They knew the bench"—knowledge. In the primal scene, knowledge has a primal value—especially in that the knowledge and the tree merge on the "mild eminence." This "quietest of places" further recalls the "house of quiet," which is later invaded by the "bad-faced stranger," the conquest of whom brings Maggie the final and ultimate knowledge. Here, where history figuratively began, is also where it ends and becomes a mythic prototype for Adam's other garden, his museum, which houses Maggie's final introjected knowledge.

Where in Book First Maggie and perhaps Fanny play a parental or maternal role, Maggie in the garden takes on quite a different role in Book Second. Here, Fanny is essentially refined out of the picture—she has "given up" both Charlotte and the Prince toward the end of Book First—and Maggie is the custodian of the garden-museum. Maggie and Adam return to the garden, and the transformation in Maggie is soon worked through.

> They were husband and wife—oh, so immensely!—as regards other persons; but after they had dropped again on their old bench . . . it was wonderfully like their having got together into some boat and paddled off from the shore where husbands and wives, luxuriant complications, made the air too tropical. In the boat they were father and daughter. . . . Why, into the bargain, for that matter—this came to Maggie—couldn't they always live, so far as they lived together, in a boat? She felt in her face, with the question, the breadth of a possibility that soothed her; they needed only *know* each other, henceforth, in the unmarried relation. . . . They *had*, after all, whatever happened, always and ever each other; each other—that was the hidden treasure and the saving truth (468–469).

The married relation between father and daughter, which had obtained in social circles since the death of Maggie's mother, and still obtains in the virtual outer world of Book Second, takes on a technically real cast in the privacy of the garden-bench of Fawns. Yet psychologically, this relation is as unreal as the other was socially unreal, because now it is "always and ever each other," as if there had been no alteration of the previous intimacy. Much as they "knew" the bench in their first meeting in the novel, here in the Edenic atmosphere they are impelled to "know" each other on an eternal basis. This of course is the same "boat" that carried Maggie's good faith at the outset of the novel. Anchored in this "boat," Adam is able then to suggest his own "shipping out" plan which was, all along, *Maggie's* idea. The boat of their mutual "knowl-edge" is, has always been, and "always and ever" will be, the foundation of Maggie's fantasy of her own omniscience; in this sense, it permits the real-world separation that forms her plan for victory. The "hidden treasure" of intimacy with her father is of a piece with all of Maggie's hidden feelings, her many metaphors express her impulse toward a violent accession to subjective power and refer to the pecuniary power which permits the social activation of her personal fantasies. Finally, the intimacy with her father is the "saving truth," because it does save the two from the possible loss of dignity, the humiliation implicit in what had happened to them, though this salvation is true only in Maggie's fantasy; what the outside world thinks is of no relevance. This intimacy, which allows the subsequent physical separation of father and daugh-ter, Maggie explains to Fanny toward the end, is what "saved" Charlotte and the Prince: "it's what—from the moment they discovered we could think at all—will have saved *them*" (523). The knowledge, Maggie imagines, in the other couple that she (and her father) could think becomes a salvation. To Maggie, only she herself thinks, as she proceeds on the assumption that her father does *not* know of her discovery. Thus, in a sense her knowledge both of the adultery and of her father is enough to "save" all concerned, but has done so while she maintains a vision, through it all, of her own innocence and su-preme sacrifice.

This is not a Christ figure, but *someone who imagines herself a Christ figure*. This is why to say that Maggie "reminds us of Christ" misses the violent psychological backwash of Maggie's imagination. Maggie has a *fantasy* of her own power, her own guiltlessness, and her own saintliness rather than actually being so. From the relatively passive figure of Book First, with Fanny doing the maternal or adult work in that Book, Maggie is transformed in Book Second into the salvationary brother figure, represented first by Christ, then by the millenarian prophets, and then by the utopians. This battery of psychologi-cally similar cultural archetypes fits hand in glove with one of the governing brother-fantasies in James's personal life. For James to have become the artist was for him the conquest of the annoying older brother, and possibly father. The primacy of fantasy-life—art-life that is—in his life brought to him the fantasy of victory, allowed the fantasies that art-life permitted to act out the victory in story after story. Finally, the archetypes and James's personal fanta-sy-dynamics appear in the great utopian surge of the turn of the century. Mag-gie, like the utopian, conceives of her aims only as benevolent and self-sacri-ficial, and these aims seek to save all with both the infinite good faith of the New World Americans and the infinite wealth of these same saints. Fawns, like the golden bowl, is given up, but consciousness is king and is the saving utopia.

The breaking of the bowl, in this context, takes on the meaning it orig-inally held in Ecclesiastes, where if "ever the golden bowl be broken," "desire shall fail. . . . Then shall the dust return to the earth as it was, and the spirit shall return unto God who gave it." While, in Maggie's fantasy, the end of the world—or the "end of such a history"—is marked by salvation for all, the apocalyptic side, which is a key feature of the Christian fantasy, explains almost all of the social or externally based behavior in the novel, as it renders this behavior conquered material to be artistically frozen in Maggie's fantasy. In a sense the social situation is destroyed in precedence of Maggie's inner victory, much as the apocalypse precedes the millenium, which, in turn, precedes final salvation. The Jews in the novel, perhaps the most enigmatic presences, find a distinct place in this apocalyptic view of Maggie's subjective action.

There are two significant Jews in the novel and both are art dealers. There is, first, Mr. Guttermann-Suess, from whom Adam buys a set of rare Damascene tiles as a kind of engagement rite that is an ostensible introduction of Charlotte to his wealth. Charlotte noted, after the taking of the "heavy cake and port wine" had rounded out the transaction, that the process took on a "touch of some mystic rite of Old Jewry" (152). Immediately after this notice appears Adam wonders "where he should see his ships burn" (152). Following his proposal to Charlotte, Adam "applied the torch" (153) for the "sacrifice of his vessels," and then "redoubled the thrust of flame." Whether the rite is of old Jewry or of new Christianity, the sense of sacrificing the most coveted 'vessels"—art, possessions, money, or women—implies the presence of both an authority and a motive for sacrificing.

Guttermann-Suess first represents a classic image of Jewish authority, a "positively lustrous young man" moving "in the bosom of his family," his progeny, "eleven little brown clear faces, yet with such impersonal old eyes astride of such impersonal old noses" (150), surrounded by "fat, ear-ringed aunts and the glossy, cockneyfied, familiar uncles, inimitable of accent and assumption, and of an attitude of cruder intention than that of the head of the firm" (150). The sense of combined age and impersonality suffusing this "tribe" (150) of children and relatives foists on Guttermann-Suess the inescapable role of patriarch. Adam and Charlotte viewing both tribe and treasure, pass by one of his tablecloths "redolent of patriarchal teas" (151). As one of the keystones of patriarchy, the 11 children offer a point of comparison between Guttermann-Suess and Adam. Charlotte, at the height of her new affair with the Prince, observes to him that "it would have taken more than ten children of mine, could I have had them—to keep our *sposi* apart." (217) Her own lack of children, she insists, is "not, at any rate, . . . my fault. There it is." (217) At the moment of his engagement Adam sees the patrimony he will never achieve. He had previously envisioned his daughter as an art object, and it is part of his literary personality that loved ones and possessions are not differentiable. Although Charlotte questions it, his motive for the engagement—the marriage, actually—is plainly given as Maggie's welfare. In short, for the retention of his own infantile identity as the supreme collector, tribute, or sacrifice is made to the principle of the family—to the Jewish patriarch.

The sacrifice Adam makes, however, is even greater than family authority, which in a sense has been sacrificed by the entire novel. Adam sacrifices an important status of mastery of Guttermann-Suess. The latter was "a perfect master of what not to say to such a personage as Mr. Verver" (151). In marrying her, Adam imagines himself initiating Charlotte to the kind of mastery Guttermann-Suess represents: he brought Charlotte to the "quite properly hard business light, . . . the room in which they had been alone with the treasure and its master . . ." (152). On one hand the dealer's mastery resides in the sheer ownership of all the "treasure," which is held in a special room apart from the "tribe;" on the other hand his business mastery hardens the "light" of the occasion by forcing Adam's check to be "equally high" to his happiness with the tiles. Rather than Charlotte being initiated, it is really Adam, who, under the aegis of the "treasure and its master," makes the "sacrifice" that admits him to *Maggie's* museum: he marries for her welfare. The Jew is the custodian of the evil, but ultimately real, world of the marketplace, which is the source of all museum objects.

Through her dealing with the other, more important, Jew in the novel, Maggie brings this marketplace into her service. Much as James's great discovery for his later, greater fiction grew out of his own failure in this marketplace, Maggie's own "failure," her purchase of the broken golden bowl, led to her own climactic discovery. In this process, moreover, the Jew is "converted," so to speak, into her own service because of a "scruple rare enough in vendors of any class, and almost unprecedented in the thrifty children of Israel" (445). Much is made of the "mysterious" nature of the merchant's action.

> He had flushed up, quite, red, with his recognition, with all his responsibility—had declared that the connection [between Charlotte, the Prince, and Maggie] must have had, mysteriously, something to do with the impulse he had obeyed [in returning to tell of the flaw] (446).

Yet only one factor is given as the cause of his action:

> at the thought of the purchaser's good faith, and charming presence, opposed to that flaw in her acquisition which would make it verily, as an offering to a loved partner, a thing of sinister meaning and evil effect, he had known conscientious, he had known superstitious visitings, had given way to a whim all the more remarkable to his own commercial mind, no doubt, from its never having troubled him in other connections. She had recognized the oddity of the adventure and left it to show for what it was (445).

This adventure, in addition to being an "oddity," was a "strange coincidence." But here the strangeness links with the mysteriousness of the motivating whim of the merchant; it is caused by the thought of the purchaser's "good faith." The mystery and the strangeness represent the distance between the cause—the good faith—and the effect—Maggie's discovery. Maggie's power is a kind of secret agent that sets new precedents even in the "thrifty children of

Israel," *especially* in these special children. Logically, the merchant's act is a breach of realism and a strain on probability. Yet psychologically, it all fits together. It is of a piece with the Prince's climactic arrival at the parlor door as Fanny breaks the bowl and with Adam's timely "decision" to "ship out" and remove Charlotte from the Prince's world. In each instance a new increment of knowledge is added to Maggie's growing store—a new victory is won. "The strangeness," she explains to the Prince, "is in what my purchase was to represent to me after I had got it home; which value came, . . . from the wonder of my having found such a friend" (428). And again, it is the "oddity of my chance, . . . that I should have been moved, in my ignorance, to go precisely to him" (428). Ignorance and innocence are defined in terms of the strangeness with which knowledge appears to it. Both the strangeness and the ignorance create the illusion of distance for both Maggie and the reader between the perception of evil in the outer "marketplace" world and the consciousness of aggression and the quest for power in herself. Coincidence and chance coincide with the fulfillment of Maggie's most important wishes. Once she introjects these coincidences, once she has "got it home," the value is recognized. And like the "wonder of my final recognition" James experienced in his nightmare, or the "wonder of consciousness in everything" James felt in his maturity, Maggie experiences the "wonder of my having found such a friend," of having brought the epitome of the marketplace, the outside world and the controlling Jew at its heart, into the service of her own subjective victory.

Thus, the Jews in this novel fill out the "millenarian" contribution to Maggie's utopian quest for an omnipotent consciousness. At the psychological root of both the millenarian and utopian fantasies, we recall, lies the more-or-less universal oral fantasy: the wish for food as the medium of total merging. Accordingly in the novel, intelligence, knowledge, conversation, words—all of these products of linguistic (oral) manufacture—become a stuffing for the containers of consciousness; they are the novel's, Maggie's, and James's main form of mental nourishment. Throughout the work, phrases and thoughts are said to be "taken in." They are "plums" and "morsels." "There was not a drop" of the Prince's conversation that Fanny "didn't . . . catch . . . for immediate bottling" (190). Food, in several important senses, is what Charlotte had before Maggie, much as she had the Prince first; much as, perhaps, older brother William and Henry Senior had mother Mary before Henry Junior. The battle between the two women, like the battle in James's dream, is undoubtedly fought on this earliest of developmental grounds. Enough money during her "hour alone" with the Prince, Charlotte tells him, is "as good as a feast" (65), yet after Maggie's victory at the end of the novel, the "empty chair at the feast" (498) is Charlotte's. When Adam told Maggie his "idea" to return to America with Charlotte, her "cup of conviction . . . overflowed" (480), while the day of stolen love at Matcham "was like a great gold cup that we must somehow drain together'' (255). After the battle is all over, Maggie has fully introjected its oral terms in one of the novel's most poignant images. Now she *imagines* Charlotte pleading with her that ''ours was everything a relation could be, filled to the brim with the wine of consciousness'' (520). The wine of consciousness—the precious Jamesian fluid—this is really the final stake of the battle. The love of Charlotte for the Prince, her ''mystifying instinct'' (88) for his language—whether it be Italian or love—her patent social sophistication and *savoir-faire*: true, Maggie seems both to lack and envy these outward attributes. But her newly won wine of consciousness dissolves them all, and that is why in the moment of triumph she imagines Charlotte making the claim for what she, Maggie, has just gained. Both Charlotte and consciousness are now really all hers—she imagines.

Various language habits of the novel testify to the universal range not only—though mainly—of Maggie's consciousness, but also of anyone's inner awareness. To ''know'' the cause of a particular event is not simply to be aware of the antecedent factors or surrounding circumstances; it is to ''know everything.'' Charlotte is not merely ignorant of what Maggie knows; Charlotte knows ''nothing.'' There is not just the lack of an illicit relationship between Charlotte and the Prince; there is ''nothing'' between them. Such absolute terms, while appearing often in the narrative stretches of the work, operate mainly in the dialogues. From this language habit emerges a key artistic modality that reinforces the development of the fantasy under consideration. Particularly, while the ordinary narrative prose reaches a consummation of Jamesian richness and density, the vocabulary of the many dialogues is sparse, riddled with absolute terms and others of comparable generality and possibility: high, poor, funny, good, right, great, splendid, magnificent. Every interchange between people turns on numerous italicized prepositions and pronouns, echoed and reemphasized phrases, with a minimum of referential meaning. Discussions are almost all emphasis and almost no specificity. The words themselves become things. Maggie is not discovering connivance or treachery; she is confronting evil with a ''very big E'' (273). Adam and Maggie do not simply settle on a nice bench; they must settle on the word ''sequestered'' as well. James's artistic machinery of renouncing and introjecting the outer world is directly expressed by his formalism. Ordinary prose, with its full, elaborate, extended metaphors, generally expresses the world of an individual, a specific area of subjective response and perception. It is, so to speak, James's real world of private retreat, true fiction, true art, the final reality. Interpersonal dialogue, however, like the theater, like social and sexual relations in general, represents activity in the outside world, the contact with the other, which carries an abiding freight of potential danger. Only brief questions can be asked, and only short, vague answers given. In the social world one does not publicly reflect or express; one parries and, occasionally, thrusts and retreats—though sometimes one "explains." This is true, it seems to me, not only of this novel, but of so much of James's most important fiction.

Much as in real life the adult faculty of *taste* reconciles our wishes with the available artistic fulfillments, taste in *The Golden Bowl* is the cornerstone of the artistic transformation of its oral fantasy into its elaborate social tapestry. The infantile psychology of the search for nourishment is translated into a verbal structure, a confrontation of arguments, words, images, and social forms, in which the stake is knowledge—the only materials admissible to adult public consumption. Much as the "master" of the treasure concludes his act with the ritual taking of the cake and wine, all of these transformed categories represent Maggie's final artistic identity in which she "takes in" the "wine of consciousness." She has taken it all in and has *become* them. In Book First, Adam is presented as the master of art: "It was all, at bottom, in him, the aesthetic principle, planted where it could burn with a cold, still flame," whose "devouring element," however, did not consume his "spiritual furniture" (139); he is thus endowed with the "blest inveteracies of taste." His acquisition of the Prince, meanwhile, brings him to the biological root of his acquisitive impulses, as he now must face "perpetual repasts" such that "he had never in his life . . . had to reckon with so much eating" (64). With the transfer of Adam's museum to Maggie's consciousness in Book Second, she overtakes this putative artistic mastery. Her conquest of the Prince, for example, is secured when "taste, in him as a touchstone, was now all at sea" (532), certainly the same Verver sea in which he could "pecuniarily float." The spiritual furniture that was presumably unaffected by the "devouring element" in Book One seems well consumed as the "human furniture" about which Maggie remarks to her father in their parting interview: "Ah, don't they look well?" Most significantly, however, Adam's "cold, still flame" reappears in Maggie's imagination in the height of passion. While imagining Charlotte's claim of the "wine of consciousness," Maggie sees, in direct apposition to that wine, "the golden flame —oh, the golden flame" (520). Like the precious wine, this still, yet golden flame is now Maggie's. Charlotte's was the flame of physical passion, but Maggie's is the "aesthetic principle," for now she has *arranged* everything according to the principle of her quest for knowledge. The flame appears, even more distinctly than it did with Adam, as the private possession of her own consciousness.

In translating the "cold, still flame" into a "golden flame," Maggie performs an artistic act paradigmatic of her overall destiny in the novel. Particularly, in subsuming the adjectives "cold" and "still" into "golden," which similarly contains the apposite "aesthetic principle," she puts a golden surface, so to speak, on the lethal paralyzing power of art—a surface of *apparent* life and love since she attributes the metaphor to the imagined passionate love of Charlotte for the Prince. For her, of course, this love is good and dead, though her act of imagining it asserts the life of her own artistic mode of functioning. Throughout the novel, this adjective functions as the overlay of artistic perfection—possibly of perfection in general—that hides and controls psychological and social violence. While the bowl itself is broken, the golden atmosphere of the novel remains as a testimony to the primacy of artistic form over the substantive it modifies in the title. One sees in this controlling adjective, even as it is a "defense," the wish for the long lost Golden Age, for something earthly yet perfect, and it offers at least the verbal formulation of perfection where chaos—"everything is terrible, *cara,* in the heart of man"—is felt to exist.

Just before Fanny is about to dash the bowl, she suggests, through her renaming of the golden bowl the "gilt cup," the psychological turpitude it is meant to cover over, for that is what Fanny calls it when Maggie points out her new evidence. In an artlessly patent moral sense, it is also a "guilt cup," and Maggie immediately and definitely agrees with Fanny in a new finality. "I mean the gilt cup!" (402). In other parts of the novel, however, this pun "works." Adam owns an old morocco case "stamped in the ineffaceable gilt with the arms of a deposed dynasty" (139), which is easily read as an oblique allusion to the Prince's deposed dynasty, guilty, and now deposed by Adam. The ever dangerous, devouring Misses Lutches are sent by Adam into "gilded insignificance" (142) as their marital assault is turned back. And Maggie imagines part of her own victory over Charlotte as the latter's struggle against the "gilt wires" (449) on her cage, against which she is "bruising her wings" (449). Maggie has destroyed, or conquered all of this guilt, by subsuming it into her "little golden personal nature" (368), likewise invented for her by her loyal artistic defender, Fanny Assingham. Gilt is the mode of the outside world, which, when introjected, is true gold.

Gold functions as a pathway to salvation. On one hand the "Golden Isles" are what Adam finds in Europe—through his two new acquisitions in the Prince and Charlotte. On the other hand the "Golden Isles" are what the Prince sees himself entering (19) when he marries Maggie. The mornings on which Adam and Maggie frequently meet are "high golden mornings" in sequestered benches and primeval gardens. The "golden chain of firm fineness" (312) around Maggie's neck is her own hold, her own pathway to control, over her two adversaries, who exist on either side of the medallion. While the Prince and Charlotte feel as if they were draining a "great gold cup" together, they feel further bound by a "mystic golden bridge" (231). At the end of the novel, when the Prince seems to be offering a final plea to Maggie of his ethical integrity—"If ever a man since the beginning of time acted in good faith—" (535), he suddenly breaks off for no apparent reason but the implied futility of finishing; Maggie sees his implication "settle," like some handful of gold dust thrown into the air—for that then Maggie showed herself, as deeply and strangely taking it. 'I see' " (535). Maggie "sees" everything through her magic golden cups, her golden atmospheres, her golden nature, her golden mornings and evenings; she was born in the golden land. Even in this last plea of the Prince the gold dust reveals his abjection even as it stops him from finally grovelling. Through this all, Maggie sees, Maggie knows.

As the surface presentation of the underlying utopian—oral and adolescent combination—fantasy becomes increasingly complex, the utopian character of the fantasy becomes more visible. The defensive illusion of the novel, is, by and large, what the novel is critically recognized to be—Maggie's winning of a social and ethical victory costing the minimum of hurt and malice, and the gaining for herself a near saintly status. This reading is the *adult disguise* of the more regressive and violent features of the work's narrative action. Reasoning backwards, so to speak, from the apparent adult issues of the work, and from the provisional understanding of James's psychology, the work's motivating fantasy becomes an adolescent masculine mobilization of the oral wish for complete incorporation of the outside world. The figure of Maggie represents this assimilative impulse in that she functions simultaneously as both mother and male-child-adolescent. As the mother, she is in the Jamesian tradition of Milly, Daisy, Isabel (Archer)—and of Minny, and, of course, James's real mother, Mary—these "m's" are already an old story in James criticism.[10] Maggie, as mother, knows and controls "everything" and in this way represents, as did James's dream, the subjective capture of home and mother in the imaginary world of the novel. As the son, however, Maggie is the "hero," the winner of the apocalyptic masculine battle with her archrival, Charlotte. This could explain Charlotte's overall role as the initiator of sexual activity, her appearing to the Prince as having "mounted, as with the whizz and the red light of a rocket" (209) when she arrived to consummate their adulterous wishes, her appearing to Maggie "launched and erect" (456) as the "bad-faced stranger," as "splended and erect" (513) when she "floats down the long vista" (513) after her last meeting with Maggie. It will explain also why Maggie is a "small erect commander" (439), why she is aiming to "penetrate" the tall pagoda in her garden with new "weapons" (294), perhaps the "bare blade" she sees before her "ten times a day" (294). It might finally explain the metaphor of Maggie's "telescope" that "gained in range" (434) once the Prince is apprised of her knowledge. Seeing is her phallic instrument, much as it is James's; it represents the taking in of outer experience and using it as the machinery of identity formation.

In withholding her confession from Father Mitchell, Maggie does away with ecclesiastical authority just as she refines Adam out of—or perhaps all the way into—the picture. After her last conversation with Charlotte, "she had done all"—she was the winner over both authority and the slightly older and more experienced rival of her own generation. Yet the proof of the totally internal nature of this victory emerges from the fact that what she is most certain of in her victory—that Charlotte remains in the complete ignorance—we readers are least certain of. The Prince toward the end is about to tell Maggie that "she knows, she knows!" (534), but Maggie interrupts him and the illusion continues on unbroken. Fantasy—Maggie's fantasy—serves for her as fact. Like the preverbal infant, she does not differentiate (in the novel) between what she imagines and what the outside world really is, and this successful psychological conflation is used to win the adolescent battle with Charlotte.

Rather than actually making love to the Prince, therefore, Maggie is always resting her head on his breast, which is the last word—perhaps figuratively as well as literally—in the novel. In one sense it is irrelevant that the Prince is a man, since his function is simply that of a putative love object for Maggie. In another sense, though, perhaps the aesthetic sense, the Prince's masculinity and Maggie's femininity are strategic reversals in gender in the service of the adult issues of the novel, so that on a fantasy level the battle with Charlotte is between two "brothers" over a woman, a fantasy which makes sense in terms of James's biography, and which is disguised by the reversals. If the Prince is regarded as a Victorian woman, his passive role becomes much clearer, while the ever present "weakness" that accompanies all descriptions of Maggie's would-be attraction to the Prince defines the realm of her own passivity—her infanthood—with respect to the "woman." In keeping with the idiom of the novel, strength in Maggie is expressed only through seeing, knowing, and imagining, which are introjected forms of sexuality. But once the introjection takes place, the fantasy content with reversed roles goes into action. Thus, normal sexual and social relationships are the artistic overlay, the defense, the key transformation that renders the utopian fantasy tractable on an adult level.

The battle of the two "men" over the one "woman" is carried into the novel's concluding conversation. Maggie somewhat rhetorically asks if Charlotte is not "splendid." The Prince repeats, "Oh, splendid!" Maggie presses for further reassurance—"That's our help, you see." The Prince dutifully fulfills her most ardent wish. "See? I see nothing but *you*." Now that the key question has been answered, and final victory over Charlotte is proclaimed, Maggie experiences a moment of what could be called tragic insight. "And the truth of it [the Prince's last remark] had, with this force, after a moment, so strangely lighted his eyes that, as for pity and dread of them, she buried her own in his breast" (548). A few moments earlier, Maggie had seen this moment with the Prince as the "reward of her efforts" to be "tasted"—the "golden fruit that shone from afar" (547). This last interchange restates the underlying idioms and issues of the novel, signalled by the terms tasted, golden, fruit, strangely, eyes, and breast. Much as the taste of the golden fruit is distanced from Maggie by "shone from afar," the truth of the Prince's abjection is distanced from the strange light in his eyes. Eyes and fruit represent the two polar components of the oral-adolescent fantasy—eyes, the adolescent sexual strength; fruit, the object to be conquered with that strength, or along with the "breast," the "reward" for heroic exercise of the eyes through seeing and knowing everything. When, in "pity and dread," Maggie blinds herself by burying her eyes in the Prince's breast, it is an act of *perception* on her part, an act the range and power of which has never before been achieved by Maggie. The suggestion is that she has at last perceived the destructive result of her efforts, though now perhaps she may safely do so, since the novel is ending.

But now we might also say that *James* might safely do so, since *his* novel is ending. Here, in this vague "strange" perception of the "truth," is perhaps the artistic equivalent of James's abiding "backache," his somatic symbol of the psychic pain he had always undergone in renouncing the outside world. To recognize the presence of such antisocial, narcissistic forces within one is in any context a supremely painful experience. Yet part of the task of being an adult human being is to find enjoyable and productive means of coping with such perception, and this was the task of James the artist. Maggie's fantasy of complete conquest, of doing "all," and James's novel of "rarest perfection" represent abiding "utopian" forces in all human beings: the wish for conditions of original satiation and calm. The fantasy further marks James's rootedness in the emotional turbulence of his age—the coincidence of the personal crisis of identity with cultural crisis. But in creating an artistic product of his fantasy, and by creating the unique kind of product he did, in which a new elaborateness of consciousness becomes both the expression of and the means of concealing the fantasy, James was able to make the "transition" into new modes of personal and cultural thought that renounce the necessity to realize the old utopian wishes yet respond to their continuing presence. The utopia that James was able to achieve in his own "great good place" is really the only utopia that is both psychologically genuine and cultural tractable. But in so achieving it, and in achieving it when and as he did, he discovered in art what many other pioneers discovered in many other enterprises—that utopia, after all, is, in spite of the wishes of the word's inventor, "delineated in words."

# Afterword

# Utopia as a Psychological and Verbal Permanence

It might seem, in the larger perspective of this essay, that the relegation of utopia to words represents its consignment to a secondary cultural order, a world of subcivilization where art is the twentieth century's real world while utopia stays in the narcissism of dreams. This is true, however, only in a strictly rational, nineteenth-century sense that conceives of reality as neatly divided between the objective and subjective experience. Much of the "transitional" character of James's work and much of the pain he experienced in developing his artistic idiom demonstrate that the division between the common notions of subjective and objective no longer prevails, and hence, that the movement of utopia from real possibility to subjective reality represents, rather than a reduction of emotional and linguistic value accorded to the idea of utopia, a major shift in the habits of its conceptualization.

Utopia as a viable idea depended on a prevailing cultural faith in some kind of workable "objective" reality, on the belief that social behavior is organizable in such a way that individual experience will be conflict-free. But this is the sense in which utopia calls for its own dissolution, since the act of social organization automatically prohibits a conflict-free situation in the individual unless the social organization is, impossibly enough, between mother and infant; and that relationship is not conflict-free either. In the normal adult world, the division between the objective social world and the subjective individual world breaks down, for neither can be conceived as independent of the other. We thus remain with the condition in which Maggie Verver functions, where there are no longer two scales of reality (the inner and the other), but one, in which inner and other are experienced as identical. The creation of this single scale as part of the twentieth-century world view is what causes the shift in our present-day conception of utopia from the older conception extant between More and Wells. It causes the shift, ironically, *back* to "Plato's" mere words.

These words, for Plato, represented straightforward intellectuality, which, in the present context, was viewed as the main adaptive machinery of the utopian fantasy. In the twentieth century, intellectuality moved closer to the world of fantasy. Both art and intellectual life, created as they both are by words or other kinds of symbolic media, came to define the single scale of twentieth-century life. Nowadays, both reality and fantasy are, in many new ways, that which is "delineated in words." There is no paradox involved here, for all that we are describing is a shift in psychological functioning toward the primacy of subjectivity and intersubjectivity in the determination of what we refer to as "reality." This primacy in contemporary epistemology shears the concept of utopia, which depended on the priority of an objective world, of its cultural relevance.

George Kateb's essay, "Utopia and the Good Life," in its direct attempt to define what is "utopian" about utopia, exemplifies through its own failure the present intellectual intractability of utopia.

> The good life is, to use the old solemn language, the contemplative life. . . . We must allow a commonplace to furnish at least the semblance of a solution of our problem; we must perhaps place all our trust in the life of the mind. . . . We could say that there is no need to mean by utopia anything more than the liberation of the higher faculties.[1]

Were it not for a heavily documented apologetic strain in utopian thought, it would probably be unfair to cite Kateb's "old solemn language" and his "commonplace" epithets as the factors undercutting his sincere attempt to articulate what "the good life" actually is. Yet we have seen that an apology is almost a necessity in many statements of the utopian wish. The apology points to the wishful nature of utopianism and represents an important feature in its system of self-obviation. The form of Kateb's utopian definition, like the form of the utopian novel, betrays a basic ambivalence. Likewise, the content of Kateb's statement, following the content of the utopian novel, is similarly boundless: "we must . . . place all our trust in the life of the mind" and in the "liberation of the higher faculties." The religious-infantile impulse of total trust is put into the service of the same utopian wish Bellamy articulated[2] at the height of Transition utopianism—the intellectual wish for omnipotence. Intellectuality, more liberated as it now is, even Kateb would acknowledge, is not utopia; it is as real as anything else in life. In another sense, intellectuality actually seeks to encompass all of life; almost any kind of professional activity involves the life of the mind in some serious way. It is only in the "old solemn language," only in the "commonplace" Transition world outlook, that the "higher faculties" are utopian. Public trust was placed in these faculties in the hope of reaching some future utopia. Kateb's present-day verbal helplessness is hardly surprising, because utopia cannot belong in a civilization that had in one sense fulfilled the utopian wish, and in another recognized that it must remain a wish.

Both the arenas of wish-fulfillment and wish-expression are verbal and in this sense both subjective. The subjectivization of the utopian fantasy in the

Transition is emblematic of the larger developments in culture and individual consciousness. Utopian ambivalence between More and Wells represented cultural ambivalence at the highest levels in religion, government, and social functioning. Cultural identities reached new degrees of turbulence and uncertainty as the inner claims of the individuals, communities, and marginal group interests began challenging long-established, externally constituted authorities, notably the church and the crown. Scientific possibility in the Transition, mobilized by intellectuals, brought these claims to their most feverish utopian pitch. Here was the zenith of reality-oriented utopianism. Yet almost in response to this other-directed upsurge, discoveries made in science (Einstein's discovery of relativity in 1905) and psychology (Freud's discovery of the unconscious in 1900) and styles created in art (notably James, but also Proust, Richardson, and after, Joyce and Faulkner) affirmed with even greater emphasis that the intrapsychic worlds created by mere words represented a more genuine basis for our ordinary conceptions of reality. These "new worlds" proved, so to speak, the impossibility of moving the utopian wish to some projected outer reality. These worlds defined utopia, as well as other objectively oriented thoughts, as *only* a fantasy.

Utopia, that is, is the name of a feeling rather than a plan for action. Exactly what feeling this is, I have sought to document in the three areas outlined at the end of Chapter 1. In psychological terms the feeling was an infantile wish for a kind of nutritional merging, mobilized by violent, undisciplined adolescent masculine energy. In more social terms, utopia is the desire to compromise the conflict of love and authority by transferring the first infantile compromise onto the relationship between the individual and the rest of mankind. The two parts of this feeling, in any case, are a wish whose early origins are largely unconscious, and an adaptive form whose *range* of later origins date, as we have seen in the various figures under discussion, from the preadolescent latency period all the way to advanced maturity. In this way, the utopian fantasy defined certain characterological constants in the individuals that permitted us to call them, provisionally, "utopian personalities." This same constellation of utopian emotions, furthermore, operated in the less personal sphere of social and political action, as well as in the more stylized and ordered, but nevertheless popular, arena of art.

The feelings present in the social and political components of the utopian fantasy were evidenced by the formation of utopian groups or movements— such as the Fabian Society and the Nationalist Movement—whose collective goals were identical to the personal wishes of the various utopians, and whose incipient collectivity represented the beginnings of the fulfillment of the utopian wish. Such groups took personal fantasies of utopians, merged them with the more traditionally collective religious fantasies, and infused them with the sense of possibility drawn from the multiplying achievements of science and technology. From these elements, Wells and the many just before and after him, created the "modern utopia." Beginning with James and somewhat before in Dostoevsky, art brought its traditional cultivations of form to the task of controlling the expanding utopian feelings. To this end, subjective consciousness itself was used as an art form, as the previous, more objectively oriented forms in the novel proved inadequate for an emotionally satisfying presentation of the utopian fantasy. While the utopian novel was the most popular art form of the day, subsequent critical and popular response to these novels viewed them unworthy of the important psychological activity of suspending disbelief, particularly because such suspension was always betrayed by the novel's compulsive infusion of material from the non-art, "real" world. The larger cultural concern with subjectivity worked in art first to express the utopian emotion in a more controlled and tractable way, but ultimately to substitute a smaller, relatively limited world of subjectivity, which creates the personal *illusion* of the totality and universality that the undisguised utopian feeling conceived of as a reality. In this sense, Maggie is someone who imagines herself a Christ figure rather than actually being one.

In all three areas into which the Transition Period was divided for study—the personal, the social and political, and the artistic—the Christian fantasy was probably the most easily recognizable element of the utopian emotion. Prior to the Christian fantasy, the classical fantasies took relatively individuated pathways to express their quest to merge with the universe. After the establishment of the Christian fantasy as a fundamental of culture, millenarian activity first began translating the literal fantasy content into social action: the implicit "now" in the fantasy's quest for salvation was made explicit. By the time More invented the word "utopia," the "new world" across the sea and the new printed word at home rendered "salvation now" worth working for. Through More, the Christian fantasy joined with the notion of its possible realization to produce the utopian fantasy, and hence the utopian emotion as we commonly know it today.

Today's familiarity with utopia, in the form of the word that exists in all the world's major languages, is certainly as great a cultural achievement as the analogous familiarity with a great work of literature or style of government. Such knowledge represents the acknowledgment of its *partial* status in the vocabulary of psychological motives, even while it retains the greatest permanence and universality any such culturally developed motive can have. In the Transition, utopia reached the verbal permanence we sense it now has, because its fantasy gave a new and compelling name to emotions which are permanent and universal in the human species.

# Notes

## Chapter 1

1. Although this particular phrase is my own, I have derived the idea from three main sources which aim to describe the larger manifestations of culture partially in terms of infantile fantasies. The work of Erik Erikson is perhaps the main source. His aim in *Childhood and Society* (1950) and in *Young Man Luther* (1958) is to determine what personality factors in both exceptional men and in the collective norms of child-rearing are reproduced and transformed in prevailing cultural generalities. Norman Cohn's *The Pursuit of the Millenium* (1957) suggests that there is a continuity between medieval millenarian fantasies and modern totalitarian phenomena. Simon O. Lesser's book, *Fiction and the Unconscious* (Boston: Beacon Press, 1957), first brought together, in a unified theoretical statement, the work of many psychological and critical studies based on Freud's early work on jokes and literature. This book analyzes at some length how fiction is to be understood as the presentation of unconscious fantasies which are "defended" by the artistic or aesthetic *form* of the works. These sources will be cited and discussed in the course of this essay.

2. The following is essentially a restatement of certain fundamental notions of psychoanalysis. For further reference, I cite several of the most important previous statements. Sigmund Freud, *The Question of Lay Analysis*, trans. James Strachey (New York, 1964); Ruth Monroe, *Schools of Psychoanalytic Thought* (New York, 1955); Calvin S. Hall, *A Primer of Freudian Psychology* (New York, 1954).

3. For a further discussion of this development in psychoanalysis, please see Chapter Three of my *Subjective Criticism* (Baltimore: Johns Hopkins University Press, 1978), "The Logic of Interpretation," which analyzes several instances of Freud's use of the "as if real" fantasy.

4. An extended discussion of how the acquisition of language is also the acquisition of the sense of self for the infant is presented in Chapter Two of my *Subjective Criticism*, "The Motivational Character of Language and Symbol Formation."

5. Erik H. Erikson, *Childhood and Society*, 2nd ed. (New York, 1950, 1963).

6. Lesser's book is the first comprehensive presentation of the "fantasy-defense" concept of literature. Chapter Five, "The Functions of Form," pp. 121–44, sets out at some length the senses in which artistic form is to be thought of as a "defense" of its fantasy content. Much of the present discussion is based on Lesser's original formulations.

7. Lesser, pp. 94–120; Erikson, *Childhood and Society*, pp. 247–51.

8. David Bleich, "The Determination of Literary Value," *Literature and Psychology* 17 (1967), pp. 19–29. The technique of this experiment was to compare the responses collected by I.A. Richards to D.H. Lawrence's poem, "Piano," with the responses of a more contemporary audience.

9. Glenn Negley and J. Max Patrick, *The Quest for Utopia* (New York, 1952), pp. 20–21.

10. Leon Edel, ed., *The Ghostly Tales of Henry James* (New Brunswick, New Jersey, 1948), p. xix. James, Edel says, "found his refuge in the great good place of the mind where he could be a simple and curious child again; or like a monk in his cell, untroubled by the material things of the world or the burdens of the flesh."

**Chapter 2**

1. Negley and Patrick, p. 252.

2. Arthur E. Morgan, *Nowhere Was Somewhere: How History Makes Utopias and How Utopias Make History* (Chapel Hill, North Carolina, 1946), p. 121.

3. Negley and Patrick, p. 252.

4. Negley and Patrick, p. 256.

5. Negley and Patrick, p. 256.

6. William Shakespeare, *The Tempest* (Baltimore: Penguin Books, 1959), p. 59 (II.i.152).

7. Erikson, *Childhood and Society*, p. 274.

8. Martin Buber, *Paths in Utopia*, trans. R.F.C. Hull (Boston, 1949, 1958), writes, p. 67: The utopian fantasy "does not float vaguely in the air, it is not driven hither and thither by the wind of caprice, it centers with architectonic firmness on something primary and original which is its destiny to build; and this primary thing is a wish."

9. Edward Surtz, S.J., and J.H. Hexter, eds., *The Complete Works of Thomas More*, vol. 4 (New Haven and London, 1965), p. xxiii.

10. Surtz and Hexter, p. xxiv.

11. Norman Cohn, *The Pursuit of the Millenium* (New York, 1957, 1961), p. 4.

12. Cohn, p. 4.

13. Cohn, p. 205.

14. Cohn, p. 205.

15. Cohn, p. 205.

16. Norman Cohn, in Sylvia L. Thrupp, *Millenial Dreams in Action: Comparative Studies in Society and History* (The Hague, 1962), p. 32.

17. Cohn first suggested the similiarity of psychological response to both the clerical "Father" and the patriarchal Jew *(The Pursuit of the Millenium*, p. 71).

18. Erikson, *Childhood and Society*, p. 337.

19. Cohn, in Thrupp, p. 39.

20. Karl Mannheim, *Ideology and Utopia* (1929), trans. Louis Wirth and Edward Shils (New York, 1963), p. 212.

21. Cohn, p. 252.

22. Cohn, p. 214.

23. Cohn, p. 210. (The quotations are Froissart's rendition of John Ball's sermon.)

24. Cohn, p. 217.

25. Victor Dupont, *L'utopie et le roman utopique dans la littérature Anglaise* (Lyon, 1941), p. 9.

26. J.L. Talmon, "Utopianism and Politics," *Commentary* XXVIII (August, 1959), p. 153.

27. John Anthony Scott, intro. More's *Utopia* (New York, 1965), p. v.

28. Surtz and Hexter, p. 127. The G.C. Richards translation of *Utopia* (first published, Oxford, Blackwells, 1923) is the basis for Surtz and Hexter's English text.

29. Surtz and Hexter, p. 69.

30. Surtz and Hexter, p. 57.

31. Surtz and Hexter, p. 99.

32. Surtz and Hexter, p. 61.

33. Surtz and Hexter, p. 71.

34. Surtz and Hexter, p. 71.

35. Frank E. Manuel, "Toward a Psychological History of Utopias," *Daedalus* XCIV (1965), p. 319.

36. Manuel, p. 293.


**Chapter 3**

1. Surtz and Hexter, p. 21.

2. Surtz and Hexter, p. 247.

3. Cohn, in Thrupp, p. 39.

4. Raymond Ruyer, *L'utopie et les utopies* (Paris, 1950), p. 37.

5. J.T. Flynn, "Why Utopias Always Fail; Condensation of Decline of the American Republic," *American Mercury* LXXXII (January, 1956), p. 149.

6. Bertrand Russell, *A History of Western Philosophy* (New York, 1945), p. 105.

7. Russell, p. 105.

8. Negley and Patrick, p. 253.

9. Negley and Patrick, p. 257.

10. Karl R. Popper, "Utopia and Violence," *Hibbert Journal* XLVI (January, 1948), p. 116.

11. Rita Falke, "Problems of Utopias," *Diogenes* 23 (1958), p. 16.

12. Falke, p. 17.

13. Falke, p. 19.

14. Ruyer, p. 39.

15. Shakespeare, *The Tempest*, II.i.153.

16. Marie Louise Berneri, *Journey Through Utopia* (Boston, 1951), p. 3.

17. Andrew Hacker, "In Defense of Utopia," *Ethics* LXV (January, 1955), p. 138.

18. It is perhaps noteworthy that at least two exceptions to this generalization are French works, the studies by Raymond Ruyer and Victor Dupont, both previously cited. Both works are untranslated, and both exhibit a critical thrust and depth of inquiry surprisingly rare in English criticism of English utopianism. Dupont's work, in fact, is the closest study I know of to a truly exhaustive treatment of the subject.

19. Oscar Wilde, "The Soul of Man Under Socialism," *Complete Works of Oscar Wilde* (London, 1948, 1966), p. 1089.

20. Frances Theresa Russell, *Touring Utopia* (New York, 1932), p. 24.

21. Lewis Mumford, *The Story of Utopias* (New York, 1922, 1962), p. 26.

22. Negley and Patrick, p. 2.

23. Negley and Patrick, p. 582.

24. Kenneth Keniston, "Alienation and the Decline of Utopia," *American Scholar* XXIX (Spring, 1960), p. 162.

25. Keniston, p. 200.

26. Paul Goodman, *Utopian Essays and Practical Proposals* (New York, 1962), p. 6.

27. Goodman, p. 9.

28. Goodman, p. 114.

29. B.F. Skinner, *Walden Two* (New York, 1948, 1962), p. 314.

30. Skinner, p. 295.

31. Skinner made this remark in response to a question from the audience after a lecture of his at Queens College in October, 1962.

32. S. Klaw, "Harvard's Skinner: the Last of the Utopians," *Harper's* CCXXVI (April, 1963), p. 47.

33. Joyce Oramel Hertzler, *The History of Utopian Thought* (New York, 1923), p. 225.

34. George Woodcock, "Utopias in the Negative," *Sewanee Review* LXIV (Winter, 1956), p. 82.

35. Woodcock, p. 83.

36. Daniel Bell, "The Study of the Future," *The Public Interest* I (Fall, 1965), pp. 119–30.

37. Bell, pp. 119, 120.

38. Bell, p. 120.

39. Herbert Marcuse, *Eros and Civilization* (New York, 1962), p. 143.

40. Alice Mary Hilton, "Cyberculture—The Age of Abundance and Leisure," *Michigan Quarterly Review* III (1964), p. 222.

41. Negley and Patrick, p. 588.

42. George Knox, "Apocalypse and Sour Utopians," *Western Humanities Review* XVI (1962), p. 11.

43. Adam Ulam, "Socialism and Utopia," *Daedalus* XCIV (Spring, 1965), p. 400.

**Chapter 4**

1. Louis J. Budd, "The Idea of Progress at the Close of the Gilded Age," *Georgia Review* XI (1957), p. 278.

2. John T. Flanagan, "The Idea of Progress: In the Era of World War I," *Georgia Review* XI (1957), p. 284.

3. Oscar Wilde, *Complete Works of Oscar Wilde* (London, 1948, 1966), p. 1089.

4. Ernest Tuveson, *Millenium and Utopia* (New York, 1949, 1964, p. 151.

5. Tuveson, p. 152.

6. George Knox, "Apocalypse and Sour Utopians," *Western Humanities Review* XVI (1962), p. 15.

7. W.H.G. Armytage, *Heavens Below; Utopian Experiments in England, 1560–1960* (London, 1961), p. 316.

8. Henry George, *Progress and Poverty* (New York, 1953), pp. 563, 564, 565. In George, the Plutarch quotation is italicized.

9. Armytage, p. 323.

10. Armytage, p. 434.

11. Allyn B. Forbes, "The Literary Quest for Utopia, 1880–1900," *Social Forces* (December, 1927), p. 181.

12. Timothy L. Smith, *Revivalism and Social Reform* (New York, 1944, 1965), p. 226. Smith's quotations are taken from *The Independent* (1851).

13. Richard Hofstadter, *Social Darwinism in American Thought* (New York, 1944, 1955), p. 110.

14. Hofstadter, p. 110.

15. Forbes, p. 180.

16. R.L. Shurter, "The Utopian Novel in America, 1888–1910," *South Atlantic Quarterly* XXXIV (April, 1935), p. 143.

17. Clinton Clarence Keeler, "The Grass Roots of Utopia: a Study of the Literature of Agrarian Revolt in America, 1880–1902," *Dissertation Abstracts* XIV (1954), p. 973 (University of Minnesota).

18. Keeler, p. 973.

19. D.H. Lawrence, *Selected Literary Criticism,* ed. Anthony Beal (New York, 1956), p. 299.

20. Lawrence, p. 299.

21. Russell B. Nye, "Populists, Progressives, and Literature: A Record of Failure," *Publications of the Michigan Academy of Science, Arts, and Letters* XIVII (1962), p. 549.

22. Oscar Wilde, *The Picture of Dorian Gray*, in *Complete Works of Oscar Wilde* (London, 1948, 1966), p. 137.

23. Bernard Bergonzi, *The Early H.G. Wells: A Study of the Scientific Romances* (Toronto, 1961), p. 12.

24. Bergonzi, p. 3.

25. Walter E. Houghton, *The Victorian Frame of Mind* (Yale University Press, 1957).

26. Houghton, p. 355.

27. Houghton, p. 310.

28. J.W. Mackail, *The Life of William Morris*, vol. 2 (London, 1899), p. 244.

29. Mackail, p. 244. Quotation is from Morris's review in *Commonweal* (June, 1889).

30. Mackail, pp. 243–44.

31. Philip Henderson, ed., *The Letters of William Morris to his Family and Friends* (London, 1950), p. xxii.

32. Henderson, p. xxii.

33. Lloyd W. Eshleman, *A Victorian Rebel: The Life of William Morris* (New York, 1940), p. 294 (italics in Eshleman). Mackail (vol. 1, p. 6) similarly suggests: "The picture which Morris draws, in 'News from Nowhere,' of this Essex county in the restored and recivilized England of a distant future, substantially represents the scene of his own boyhood."

34. Eshleman, p. 7.

35. Holbrook Jackson, *William Morris, Craftsman-Socialist* (London, 1908), p. 9

36. Jackson, p. 9.

37. Jackson, p. 9.

38. Jackson, p. 9.

39. Jackson, p. 10.

40. Mackail, vol. 1, p. 85. Quotes letter of 11 November 1855.

41. Mackail, vol. 2, p. 346.

42. Henderson, p. xxiv.

43. Mackail, vol. 2, p. 343.

44. Mackail, vol. 1, p. 63. Quotation is from a letter of Burne-Jones.

45. Mackail, vol. 1, p. 63. Quotation is from another letter to Burne-Jones.

46. Mackail, vol. 1, p. 63.

47. Eshleman (pp. 9–13) relates an anecdote which, if true, offers important documentation for Morris's basic sense of estrangement from his family and subsequently from society. At the age of about six, he and his sister Jennie awaited the return of Father for dinner. After Jennie identified Father in the distance, William responded that it was not Father, but "Saladin, the Turkish heretic, and I am Richard of the Lion Heart, waiting to fell him with my strong iron sword and good long bow." Then Jennie sprang forth to greet him while William "came

scrambling after her . . . and his feet tripping over one another at every third step, until he went tumbling head over heels on the greensward.'' Right through until dinner, Jennie held Father's attention, while ''naughty and wicked'' William was reproved for not washing before dinner: ''Upstairs William went, feeling very certain that there was no justice in the world.'' Subsequently, on going to bed: ''It was a long time before the little boy relaxed and softly cried himself to sleep. Only in his dreams could he realize to the full his mental and physical prowess, and ride forth, a noble knight in shining armour, to help right the injustices of the world.'' Ordinarily, perhaps, the aggressive wish would be resolved either in playful acting out or in some manifestation of father's love. Neither resolution was possible, it would seem, and ''injustice'' prevailed, along with the aggressive wish.

48.  George Bernard Shaw, *William Morris as I Knew Him (New York, 1936), p. 39.*

49.  Mackail, vol. 2, p. 344.

50.  Bruce Glasier, *William Morris and the Early Days of the Socialist Movement* (London, 1921), p. 168.

51.  Mackail (vol. 1, p. 225) notes that for Morris ''the love of things had all the romance and passion that is generally associated with the love of persons only.'' He quotes (vol. 2, p. 343) a remark of Burne-Jones's: ''If you have got one of his books in your hands for a minute, he'll take it away from you as if you were hurting it, and show it to you himself.'' ''The mere handling of a beautiful thing,'' Mackail comments, ''seemed to give him intense physical pleasure.''

52.  Jackson (p. 56) identifies this ambivalence as the source of Morris's utopianism: ''His consciousness was utopian. He lived a double life, one amidst the turmoil and chaos of a society which antagonized him at every point, and the other, his real life, in a wondrous realm of happy fellowship and bright colour, a peaceful sanctuary full of the activities of useful work joyfully performed and steeped in a large and reflective leisure.''

53.  This unattainable feast appears at the conclusion of *News from Nowhere,* where the hero-dreamer, William Guest, fades into invisibility—and into reality, as the consummation of his ''vision'' begins.

54.  Mackail, vol. 1, p. 218.

55.  Arthur Ernest Morgan, *Edward Bellamy* (New York, 1944), p. 180. This material, Morgan indicates, was written in Bellamy's twenties, and is taken from certain of his unpublished papers.

56.  Morgan (p. 145) is quoting material from Mason A. Green's unpublished biography of Bellamy.

57.  Morris's objection to Bellamy's military idiom could be due to the latter's expression of impulses Morris needed to keep latent.

58.  Morgan, p. 9.

59.  Morgan, p. 31.

60.  Sylvia E. Bowman, *The Year 2000: A Critical Biography of Edward Bellamy* (New York, 1958), p. 17.

61.  Morgan, p. 25.

62.  Morgan, p. 25.

63. Morgan, p. 20.

64. Bowman, p. 17.

65. Morgan, p. 68. Bowman (p. 16) similarly observes that after Edward's brother Packer died in 1868, "Edward was thenceforth to be in more ways than one his mother's boy. . . . Despite his reticence, he was to be more in rapport with his mother than anyone else, and all of his life he was to spend hours conversing with her about books and ideas—and this, perhaps, was as it should have been, for she had helped to form his interests."

66. Morgan, p. 27.

67. Edward Bellamy, *The Religion of Solidarity,* ed. Arthur Morgan (Yellow Springs, Ohio, 1940), p. 41.

68. Bellamy, *The Religion of Solidarity,* p. 40.

69. Some further discussion of this feminine rescue is found in my essay, "Eros and Bellamy," *American Quarterly* XVI (1964), p. 458. The transformation of Julian's life from past to future is acted out in terms of his feminine attachments.

70. Edward Bellamy, "A Positive Romance," *The Blindman's World and Other Stories* (New York, 1898), p. 306.

71. Morgan, p. 41.

72. Morgan, p. 53. Quoted from an unpublished, third person autobiography.

73. Morgan, p. 186. Quoted from same unpublished source indicated in footnote 72 above.

74. Morgan, p. 21. Bellamy's letter of 21 October 1886. His father died on 16 November 1886.

75. Morgan, p. 411.

**Chapter 5**

1. Negley and Patrick, pp. 20–21.

2. Particularly, the situation of the millenarian uprisings, where mob ethics overrule the usual social processes.

3. Robert DeMaria, *From Bulwer-Lytton to George Orwell: the Utopian Novel in England, 1870–1950* (New York, 1959), p. 411 (Columbia University dissertation).

4. Richard Gerber, *Utopian Fantasy: a Study of English Utopian Fiction since the End of the Nineteenth Century* (London, 1955), p. 123.

5. Herbert Read, *English Prose Style* (London, 1928), p. 146.

6. Berneri, p. 219.

7. Berneri, p. 219.

8. Ruyer, p. 13.

9. Dupont, p. 714.

10. Berneri, p. 219.

11. Quoted by Gerber, p. 81.

12.  H.G. Wells, *A Modern Utopia* (London, 1905), pp. 10, 11.

13.  Gerber, p. 81.

14.  Berneri, p. 218.

15.  DeMaria, p. 1.

16.  DeMaria, p. 411.

17.  Dupont, p. 7.

18.  Bleich, "The Determination of Literary Value" pp. 19–29. (Footnote 8, chapter 2, above.)

**Chapter 6**

1.  Norman Nicholson, *H.G. Wells* (London, 1950), p. 54.

2.  George Bernard Shaw, in *New Statesman and Nation* (1946); quoted by Vincent Brome, *H.G. Wells, a Biography* (London, 1951), p. 5.

3.  Brome, p. 110.

4.  Brome, p. 110.

5.  Bergonzi, p. 166.

6.  Bergonzi, p. 166.

7.  Gordon N. Ray, ed., *The History of Mr. Polly* by H.G. Wells (Boston, 1960), p. xxi.

8.  Nicholson, p. 62n.

9.  Margaret Cole, *The History of Fabian Socialism* (New York, 1964), p. 23.

10.  Bergonzi, p. 173. Nicholson (p. 66) likewise notes in Wells a "tendency to idealise adolescence. What Wells was seeking between man and woman was the boyhood dream of romance; through all the hopes and ecstasies and disillusionments of adult love he was looking nostalgically for a boy's vision." Professional and domestic life for Wells were both adolescent.

11.  Brome, p. 126.

12.  Ray (p. xviii), in noting that "Wells hated the upper class, the late Victorian 'Establishment,' " points to the conscious feeling Wells experienced. That this hatred of Wells's was at least ambivalent is suggested by his attachment to elitism.

13.  Brome, p. 14.

14.  H.G. Wells, *Experiment in Autobiography* (New York, 1934), p. 44.

15.  Wells, *Experiment,* p. 36.

16.  Wells, *Experiment,* p. 37.

17.  Wells, *Experiment,* p. 37.

18.  Wells's criticism of his father *(Experiment,* p. 153ff.) as a "man with a singular distaste for contention or holding his own in the world" suggests why the younger Wells might have *wanted* his father to entertain secret celestial aspirations.

19.  Wells, from the typescript of preface to Russian translation of his selected works (Illinois). Quoted in Ray, p. xvi-xvii.

20. Cole, p. 123.

21. Wells *(Experiment,* pp. 156–57) recounts how, like Polly, his father and brother were paralyzed by the small shop and forever consigned to mediocrity.

22. Leon Edel and Gordon N. Ray, *Henry James and H.G. Wells: A Record of Their Friendship, Their Debate on the Art of Fiction, and Their Quarrel* (Urbana, Illinois, 1958), p. 18.

23. Edel and Ray, p. 18.

24. Wells, *Experiment,* p. 410.

25. Edel and Ray, p. 19.

26. Edel and Ray, p. 18.

27. Edel and Ray, p. 134. Taken from "a talk given [by Wells] to the Times Book Club in 1911 on 'The Scope of the Novel' " (Edel and Ray, p. 131).

28. Edel and Ray, p. 263. James's letter of 6 July 1915.

29. Quoted by Edel and Ray, p. 29.

30. Edel and Ray, p. 18.

31. Edel and Ray, p. 18.

32. Edel and Ray, p. 61. James's letter of 20 November 1899.

33. Edel and Ray, p. 105. James's letter of 19 November 1905.

34. Edel and Ray, p. 115. James's letter of 8 November 1906.

35. Edel and Ray, p. 121. James's letter of 14 October 1909.

36. Edel and Ray, p. 27.

37. Edel and Ray, p. 114. James's letter of 8 November 1906.

38. Edel and Ray, pp. 94–95. James's letter of 24 January 1904.

39. Edel and Ray, pp. 182–83. James's essay, "The Younger Generation," originally appeared in *"The Times Literary Supplement* 19 March and 2 April 1914, pp. 133–134 and 137–158" (Edel and Ray, p. 178n).

40. Edel and Ray, pp. 80–81. James's letter of 7 October 1902.

41. Edel and Ray, p. 103–4. James's letter of 19 November 1905.

42. Edel and Ray, p. 32. Quotation is from a James letter to Edmund Gosse.

43. Henry James, *A Small Boy and Others* (New York, 1913), p. 3.

44. Percy Lubbock, ed., *The Letters of Henry James,* vol. 2 (New York, 1920), p. 15. Letter to J.B. Pinker, James's literary agent, 20 May 1904.

45. Henry James, *The Golden Bowl* (New York: Evergreen Books, 1959), p. 470.

46. Quoted from Van Wyck Brooks, *The Pilgrimage of Henry James* (New York, 1925), p. 152. Primary source not given.

47. Edel, *Tales,* p. 568.

48. Edel, *Tales,* p. 567.

49. Edel, *Tales*, "The Great Good Place," p. 576.

50. Edel, *Tales*, p. 570.

51. Edel, *Tales*, "The Great Good Place," p. 593.

52. Edel, *Tales*, "The Great Good Place," p. 596.

53. Edel, *Tales*, "The Great Good Place," p. 596.

54. F.O. Matthiessen and Kenneth B. Murdock, eds., *The Notebooks of Henry James* (New York, 1961), p. 131.

55. Matthiessen and Murdock, p. 188.

56. Matthiessen and Murdock, p. 188.

57. Lubbock, vol. 2, p. 15. Letter of 20 May 1904.

58. Leon Edel, *Henry James: The Untried Years* (New York, 1953), pp. 180–81.

59. Edel, *The Untried Years*, p. 181.

60. Edel, *The Untried Years*, p. 57.

61. James, *Small Boy*, p. 347.

62. Edel, *The Untried Years*, p. 75.

63. James, *Small Boy*, p. 346.

64. Quoted from Edel, *The Untried Years*, p. 41.

65. James, *The Golden Bowl*, p. 535.

66. Quoted by Edel, *Tales*, p. xxv.

67. Leon Edel, private communication, 1962.

## Chapter 7

1. Wells, *A Modern Utopia* p. 12. Hereinafter page references to this work will appear in parentheses following the quoted material.

2. For example, "Practically the whole of the responsible rule of the world is in their hands; all our head teachers and disciplinary heads of colleges, our judges, barristers, employers of labour beyond a certain limit, practising medical men, legislators, must be *samurai,* and all the executive committees, and so forth, that play so large a part in our affairs are drawn by lot exclusively from them" (278).

3. While the sojourn in the wilderness is the heart of the religion, normal daily life demands, among other things, that the *samurai* "must read aloud from the Book of the Samurai for at least ten minutes every day" (297). Such "bible" study is part of an elaborate system of personal rituals which lend "modern utopian" life an underlying religious tonality.

4. Wells wrote late in life *(Experiment,* p. 564) that "The idea [of the samurai] was as good as the attempt to realize it was futile. . . . No part of my career rankles so acutely in my memory with the conviction of bad judgment, gusty impulse and real inexcusable vanity, as that storm in the Fabian tea-cup."

5. Italics in *A Modern Utopia.*

6. Edel and Ray, p. 104. James's letter of 19 November 1905.

7. The entire passage is in italics in *A Modern Utopia*.

**Chapter 8**

1. Stephen Spender, in F.W. Dupee, ed., *The Question of Henry James* (New York, 1945), p. 283.

2. Oscar Cargill, *The Novels of Henry James* (New York, 1961), p. 434.

3. Caroline Gordon, "Mr. Verver, Our National Hero," *The Sewanee Review* LXIII (Winter, 1955), p. 46.

4. Frederick C. Crews, *The Tragedy of Manners* (New Haven, 1957), p. 107.

5. Crews, p. 81.

6. James, *Small Boy,* p. 347.

7. James, *The Golden Bowl,* p. 101. Hereinafter page references to this work will appear in parentheses following the quoted material.

8. Austin Warren, in Naomi Lebowitz, ed., *Discussions of Henry James* (Boston, 1962), p. 103. Warren's remarks were first published in *The Kenyon Review* (Autumn, 1943).

9. Joseph A. Ward, *The Imagination of Disaster and Evil in the Fiction of Henry James* (Lincoln, Nebraska, 1961), p. 151. Crews (p. 102) likewise observes that "the bowl symbolizes the defective marriage between Maggie and the Prince."

10. See, for example, John W. Schroeder, "The Mothers of Henry James," *American Literature* XXII (January, 1951), pp. 424–31. Schroeder points to a series of "mothers," not necessarily beginning with the letter "m," appearing in the four "ghostly tales," "The Great Good Place," "The Beast in the Jungle," "The Jolly Corner," and "Crapy Cornelia."

**Afterword**

1. George Kateb, "Utopia and the Good Life," *Daedalus* XCIV (1965), pp. 468, 472.

2. See, for example, Edward Bellamy, *Looking Backward* (New York: Signet Classics, 1960), p. 136: Dr. Leete explains to Julian that citizens of Boston in the year 2000 look forward to the time, after the labor years are over, when "we can fully devote ourselves to the higher exercise of our faculties, the intellectual and spiritual enjoyments and pursuits which alone mean life."

# Works Cited and Consulted

### I. Utopianism in General

Adams, Robert P. "The Social Responsibilities of Science in *Utopia, New Atlantis,* and After." *JHI* X (1949): 374–98.

Armytage, W.H.G. *Heavens Below: Utopian Experiments in England, 1560–1960.* London, 1961.

Balz, A.G. "Modern Faith and the Utopian Fallacy." *Humanistic Studies in Honor of John Calvin Metcalf,* by various authors. Charlottesville, Virginia, 1941.

Beer, M. *General History of Socialism and Social Struggles.* Vol. 2. London, 1957. See especially "English Utopians" (pp. 147–80); "French Utopias and Social Criticism" (pp. 193–217); "Italian Utopias" (pp. 181–92).

Bell, Daniel. "The Study of the Future." *The Public Interest* 1 (Fall, 1965): 119–30.

Berneri, Marie Louise. *Journey through Utopia.* Boston, 1951.

Bernstein, S. "From Utopianism to Marxism." *Science and Society* XVI, no. 1 (1950): 58–67.

Bestor, Arthur Eugene. "Search for Utopia." *Heritage of the Middle West.* ed. J.J. Murray. Norman, Oklahoma, 1958.

Bloch, Ernst. *Das Prinzip Hoffnung.* 5 vols. Frankfurt, 1959.

Bloch-Laine, Francois. "The Utility of Utopias for Reformers." *Daedalus* XCIV (Spring, 1965): 419–36.

Bloomfield, P. "Eugenics of the Utopians: the Utopia of the Eugenists." *Eugenic Review* XL (January, 1949): 191–98.

Bowes, G.K. "Doom of Social Utopias: a Study of Population." *Hibbert Journal* XXXV (January, 1937): 161–75.

Bridges, H.J. "Don't Expect Utopia Overnight." *Humanity on Trial.* New York, 1941.

Brinton, Crane. "Utopia and Democracy." *Daedalus* XCIV (Spring, 1965): 348–66.

Buber, Martin. *Paths in Utopia.* Trans. R.F.C. Hull. Boston, 1949, 1958.

Budd, Louis J. "The Idea of Progress at the Close of the Gilded Age." *GaR* XI (1957): 278–84.

Calverton, Victor Francis. *Where Angels Dared to Tread.* New York, 1941.

Carpenter, Frederic I. " 'The American Myth': Paradise (to be) Regained." *PMLA* LXXIV (1959): 599–606.

Carr, E.H. "Utopia and Reality: a Conservative View." *Modern Political Thought.* Ed. W. Ebenstein. 2nd ed. New York, 1960.

Carter, Everett. "The Idea of Progress: In Recent Times." *GaR* XI (1957): 291–97.

Cheney, B. "Christianity and the Tragic Vision—Utopianism, USA." *SR* LXIX (1961): 515–33.

Clarke, I.F. "The Nineteenth Century Utopia." *QR* CCXCVI (1958): 80–91.

Cohn, Norman. *The Pursuit of the Millennium.* New York, 1957, 1961.

Cole, Margaret. *The Story of Fabian Socialism.* New York, 1964.

Cornu, A. "German Utopianism: True Socialism." *Science and Society* XII, no. 1 (1948): 97–112.

Dahrendorf, R. "Out of Utopia: Toward a Reorientation of Sociological Analysis." *American Journal of Sociology* LXIV (Summer, 1958): 115–27.

DeMaria, Robert. *From Bulwer-Lytton to George Orwell: the Utopian Novel in England, 1870–1950.* New York, 1959. Columbia University dissertation.

Dubos, René. *The Dreams of Reason: Science and Utopias.* New York, 1961.

Dupont, Victor. *L'utopie et le roman utopique dans la littérature Anglaise.* Lyon, 1941.

Falke, Rita. "Problems of Utopias." *Diogenes* 23 (1958): 14–22.

Fisher, Robert Thaddeus. "A Historical Study of the Educational Theories Contained in the Classical Utopias." *DA* XXI (1960): 310–11.

Flanagan, John T. "The Idea of Progress: In the Era of World War I." *GaR* (1957): 284–90.

Flynn, J.T. "Why Utopias Always Fail." *American Merc* LXXXII (January, 1956): 149–55.

Forbes, Allyn B. "The Literary Quest for Utopia, 1880–1900." *Social Forces* VI (December, 1927): 179–89.

Franzen, Erich. "Das Drama zwischen Utopie und Wirklichkeit." *Merkur* XIV (1960): 739–56.

Frye, Northrop. "Varieties of Literary Utopias." *Daedalus* XCIV (Spring, 1965): 323–47.

Garnett, M. "Reality and Utopia." *Hibbert Journal* XXXVIII (July, 1940): 480–88.

George, Henry. *Progress and Poverty.* New York, 1953.

Gerber, Richard. *Utopian Fantasy: A Study of English Utopian Fiction since the end of the Nineteenth Century.* London, 1955.

Golffing, F. "Notes Towards a Utopia." *PR* XXVII (1960): 514–25.

Goodman, Paul. *Utopian Essays and Practical Proposals.* New York, 1962.

Goodman, Paul and Goodman, Percival. *Communitas.* New York, 1960.

Gordon, Manya. "Utopia, or Perfection without Freedom." *How to Tell Progress from Reaction.* New York, 1944.

Hacker, Andrew. "In Defense of Utopia." *Ethics* LXV (January, 1955): 135–38.

Hertzler, Joyce Oramel. *The History of Utopian Thought.* New York, 1923.

Hilton, Alice Mary. "Computers and Cyberculture." *Michigan Quarterly Review* III (1964): 217–29.

Hofstadter, Richard. *Social Darwinism in American Thought.* New York, 1944, 1955.

Huxley, Aldous. "Boundaries of Utopia." *VQR* VII (January, 1931): 47–54.

Jackson, Holbrook. *Dreamers and Dreams.* London, 1948.

Jones, Joseph. "Utopias as Dirge." *AmQ* II (Fall, 1950): 214–26.

Jouvenel, Bertrand de. "Utopia for Practical Purposes." *Daedalus* XCIV (Spring, 1965): 437–53.

Kateb, George. *Utopia and its Enemies.* New York, 1963.

———. "Utopia and the Good Life." *Daedalus* XCIV (Spring, 1965): 454–73.

Kaul, A.N. *The American Vision: Actual and Ideal Societies in Nineteenth Century Fiction.* New Haven, 1963.

Keeler, Clinton Clarence. "The Grass Roots of Utopia: A Study of the Literature of Agrarian Revolt in America, 1880–1902." *DA* XIV (1954): 973.

Keniston, Kenneth. "Alienation and the Decline of Utopia." *Am Schol* XXIX (Spring, 1960): 161–200.

Klaw, S. "Harvard's Skinner: the Last of the Utopians." *Harper's* CCXXVI (April, 1963): 45–51.

Knox, George. "Apolcalypse and Sour Utopians." *WHR* XVI (1962): 11–22.

Laidler, Harry Wellington. "Significance of Utopianism—Modern Utopian Writers." *Social-Economic Movements.* New York, 1947.

Liljegren, S.B. *Studies on the Origin and Early Tradition of English Utopian Fiction.* Uppsala, Sweden, 1961.

Lockwood, Maren. "The Experimental Utopia in America." *Daedalus* XCIV (Spring, 1965): 401–18.

Longtin, Ray C. "The Image of Paradise in Oregon." *DA* XVI (1956): 2151–52.

Mack, Mary P. "The Fabians and Utilitarianism." *JHI* XVI (1953): 76–88.

Mannheim, Karl. *Ideology and Utopia.* Trans. Louis Mirth and Edward Shils. New York, 1963.

Manuel, Frank E. "Toward a Psychological History of Utopias." *Daedalus* XCIV (Spring, 1965): 293–322.

Marriott, J.W. "Modern Utopias in Conflict." *Hibbert Journal* XIII (October, 1914): 124–37.

Mead, Margaret. "Towards More Vivid Utopias." *Science* CXXVI (1957): 957–61.

More, Thomas. *Utopia,* trans. G.C. Richards. *The Complete Works of Thomas More.* Vol. 4. Eds. Edward Surtz, S.J., and J.H. Hexter. New Haven and London, 1965.

Morgan, Arthur E. *Nowhere was Somewhere: How History Makes Utopias and How Utopias Make History.* Chapel Hill, North Carolina, 1946.

Morton, Arthur Leslie. *The English Utopia.* London, 1952.

Mumford, Lewis. *The Story of Utopias.* New York 1922, 1962.

Negley, Glenn, and Patrick, J. Max. *The Quest for Utopia: an Anthology of Imaginary Societies.* New York, 1952.

Nye, Russell B. "Populists, Progressives, and Literature: a Record of Failure." *PMASAL* XLVII (1962): 549–63.

Ozmon, Howard Augustine, Jr. "Educational Utopias." *DA,* XXIII (1961), 1628.

Parrington, Vernon Louis, Jr. *American Dreams, a Study of American Utopias.* New York, 1947.

Popper, Karl R. "Utopia and Violence." *Hibbert Journal* XLVI (January, 1948): 109–16.

Reagan, Michael D. "Washington Should Pay Taxes to the Poor." *New York Times Magazine* (20 February 1966): 24–25, 84, 88, 90.

Riesman, David. "Some Observations on Community Plans and Utopia." *Individualism Reconsidered.* Glencoe, Illinois, 1954.

Russell, Bertrand. *A History of Western Philosophy.* New York, 1945.

Russell, Frances Theresa. *Touring Utopia.* New York, 1932.

Ruyer, Raymond. *L'utopie et les utopies.* Paris, 1950.

Schmerl, Rudolf Benjamin. "Reason's Dream: Anti-Totalitarian Themes and Techniques of Fantasy." *DA* XXI (1961): 2298–99.

Shklar, Judith. "The Political Theory of Utopia: From Melancholy to Nostalgia." *Daedalus* XCIV (Spring, 1965): 367–81.

Shurter, R.L. "The Utopian Novel in America, 1888–1910." *SAQ* XXXIV (April, 1935): 137–44.

Skinner, B.F *Walden Two.* New York, 1948, 1962.

Smith, John Maynard. "Eugenics and Utopia." *Daedalus* XCIV (Spring, 1965): 487–505.

Smith, Timothy L. *Revivalism and Social Reform in Mid-Nineteenth Century.* New York, 1957, 1965.

Snow, T.C. "Imagination in Utopia." *Hibbert Journal* XI (July, 1913): 751–65.

Sorenson, M. Susan. "An Existential Utopia." *Minnesota R.* IV (Spring, 1964): 357–68.

Stevick, Philip. "The Limits of Anti-Utopia." *Criticism* VI (1964): 233–45.

Surtz, E. "Link between Pleasure and Communism in *Utopia.*" *MLN* LXX (Fall, 1955): 90–93.

Talmon, J.L. "Utopianism and Politics." *Com* XXVIII (August, 1959): 149–54.

Thrupp, Sylvia L. *Millennial Dreams in Action: Comparative Studies in Society and History.* The Hague, 1962.

Tuveson, Ernest L. *Millennium and Utopia.* Berkeley, 1949.

Ulam, Adam. "Socialism and Utopia." *Daedalus* XCIV (Spring, 1965): 382–400.

Walsh, Chad. *From Utopia to Nightmare.* New York, 1962.

Wilde, Oscar. "The Soul of Man Under Socialism." *Complete Works of Oscar Wilde.* London, 1948, 1966.

## II. Literature, Psychology and Social Science

Berger, Harry Jr. "The Ecology of the Mind: The Concept of Period Imagination—An Outline Sketch." *CRAS* VIII (1964): 409–34.

Bleich, David. "The Determination of Literary Value." *L&P* XVII (1967): 19–30.

Edel, Leon. *The Modern Psychological Novel.* New York, 1955.

Ehrenzweig, Anton. "A New Psychoanalytical Approach to Aesthetics." *BJA* II (1962): 301–17.

Ellis, J.M. "Great Art: A Study of Meaning." *BJA* III (1963): 165–71.

Erikson, Erik H. *Childhood and Society.* New York, 1950.

———. *Insight and Responsibility.* New York, 1964.

———. *Young Man Luther.* New York, 1958.

Fraiberg, Louis B. "The Use of Psychoanalytical Ideas by Literary Critics." *DA* XVII (1957): 1336–37.

Freud, Sigmund. *Basic Writings.* Trans. and ed. A.A. Brill. New York, 1938.

———. *Beyond the Pleasure Principle.* Trans. James Strachey. New York, 1959.

———. *Civilization and Its Discontents.* Trans. James Strachey. New York, 1962.

———. *Collected Papers.* 5 vols. Trans. Jean Riviere. New York, 1959.

———. *Group Psychology and the Analysis of the Ego.* Trans. James Strachey. New York, 1960.

———. *Leonardo da Vinci and a Memory of his Childhood.* Trans. Alan Tyson. New York, 1964.

———. *The Ego and the Id.* Trans. James Strachey. New York, 1960.

———. *The Future of an Illusion.* Trans. W.D. Robson-Scott. New York, 1960.

Gombrich, E.H. "Freud's Aesthetics." *Encounter* XXVI, no. 1 (January, 1966): 30–40.

Harding, D.W. "Psychological Processes in the Reading of Fiction." *BJA* II (1962): 133–47.

Hoffman, Frederick J. *Freudianism and the Literary Mind.* Baton Rouge, Louisiana, 1945.

Huizinga, Johan. *Homo Ludens.* Boston, 1955.

Jessup, Bertram. "What is Great Art?" *BJA* II (1962): 26–35.

Kazin, Alfred. "Psychoanalysis and Contemporary Literary Culture." *Psychoanalysis and the Psychoanalytic Review* XLV, i–ii (1958): 41–51.

Kris, Ernst. *Psychoanalytic Explorations in Art.* New York, 1952.

Lesser, Simon O. *Fiction and the Unconscious.* Boston, 1957.

Marcuse, Herbert. *Eros and Civilization: A Philosophical Inquiry into Freud.* Boston, 1955.

Munroe, Ruth L. *Schools of Psychoanalytic Thought.* New York, 1955.

Rieff, Philip. *Freud: The Mind of the Moralist.* New York, 1959.

Rosenberg, Harold. "Literary Form and Social Hallucination." *PR* XXVII (1960): 638–51.

Ruitenbeek, Hendrik M., ed. *Psychoanalysis and Literature.* New York, 1964.

Weisinger, Herbert. "The Hard Vision of Freud." *The Agony and the Triumph.* East Lansing, Michigan, 1964.

## III. Edward Bellamy

Bellamy, Edward. *Dr. Heidenhoff's Process.* London, 1884.

———. *Equality.* 2nd ed. New York, 1897.

———. *Looking Backward.* New York, 1960.

———. *The Blindman's World and Other Stories.* Boston and New York, 1898.

———. *The Religion of Solidarity,* ed. Arthur Morgan (Yellow Springs, Ohio, 1940).

Blau, Joseph L. "Bellamy's Religious Motivation for Social Reform: A Review Article." *R Rel* XXI (March, 1957): 156–66.

Bleich, David. "Eros and Bellamy." *AmQ* XVI (1964): 444–59.

Bowman, Sylvia E. "Bellamy's Missing Chapter." *NEQ* XXXI (March, 1958): 47–65.

———. *Edward Bellamy Abroad: An American Prophet's Influence.* New York, 1962.

———. *The Year 2000: A Critical Biography of Edward Bellamy*. New York, 1958.

Franklin, J.H. "Edward Bellamy and the Nationalist Movement." *NEQ* XI (December, 1938): 739–72.

Howells, W.D. "Edward Bellamy." *Criticism and Fiction and Other Essays*. Eds. C.M. Kirk and R. Kirk. New York, 1959.

Madison, C.A. "Edward Bellamy: Social Dreamer." *NEQ* XV (Summer, 1942): 444–66.

Morgan, Arthur Ernest. *Edward Bellamy*. New York, 1944.

———. *Plagiarism in Utopia: A Study of the Continuity of the Utopian Tradition*. Yellow Springs, Ohio, 1944.

———. *The Philosophy of Edward Bellamy*. New York, 1945.

Sadler, Elizabeth. "One Book's Influence: Edward Bellamy's 'Looking Backward.' " *NEQ* XVIII (December, 1944): 530–55.

Schiffman, Joseph. "Edward Bellamy's Altruistic Man." *AmQ* VI (1954): 195–209.

———. "Edward Bellamy's Religious Thought." *PMLA* LXVIII (1953): 716–32.

Shurter, R.L. "The Literary Work of Edward Bellamy." *AL* V (1933): 229–34.

———. "The Writing of *Looking Backward*." *SAQ* XXXVIII (1939): 255–61.

## IV. William Morris

Eshleman, Lloyd W. *A Victorian Rebel: The Life of William Morris*. New York, 1940.

Glasier, J.B. *William Morris and the Early Days of the Socialist Movement*. London, 1921.

Godwin, E. & S. *Warrior Bard*. London, 1948.

Helmholz-Phelan, A. von. *The Social Philosophy of William Morris*. Durham, North Carolina, 1927.

Henderson, Philip, ed. *The Letters of William Morris to his Family and Friends*. London, 1950.

Jackson, Holbrook. *William Morris, Craftsman-Socialist*. London, 1908.

Kegel, Charles H. "William Morris and the Religion of Fellowship." *WHR* XII (1958): 233–40.

Mackail, J.W. *The Life of William Morris*. 2 vols. London, 1899.

Morris, William. *A Dream of John Ball*. London, 1888.

———. *News from Nowhere*. London, 1891.

Shaw, George Bernard. *William Morris as I Knew Him*. New York, 1936.

Thompson, E.P. *William Morris: Romantic to Revolutionary*. London, 1955.

## V. H.G. Wells

Bergonzi, Bernard. *The Early H.G. Wells: A Study of the Scientific Romances*. Toronto, 1961.

Brome, Vincent. *H.G. Wells, A Biography*. London, 1951.

Edel, Leon, and Ray, Gordon. *Henry James and H.G. Wells: A Record of Their Friendship, Their Debate on the Art of Fiction, and Their Quarrel*. Urbana, Illinois, 1958.

Nicholson, Norman. *H.G. Wells*. London, 1950.

Orwell, George. "Wells, Hitler, and the World State." *Golden Horizon*. Ed. Cyril Connolly. New York, 1953.

Ray, Gordon N., ed. and intro. *The History of Mr. Polly,* by H.G. Wells. Boston, 1960.

Wells, H.G. *A Modern Utopia*. London, 1905.

———. *Experiment in Autobiography*. New York, 1934.

## VI. Henry James

Anderson, Quentin. "Henry James and the New Jerusalem." *KR* VIII (1946): 515–66.

Bantock, G.H. "Morals and Civilization in Henry James." *Cambridge J* VII (December, 1953): 159–81.

Bass, Eben Edward. "Ethical Form in the Fiction of Henry James." *DA* XXIII (1962): 1015.

Bayley, John. *The Characters of Love: A Study in the Literature of Personality.* New York, 1960.

Bewley, Marius. "Henry James and the Economic Age." *The Eccentric Design.* New York, 1959.

Brooks, Van Wyck. *The Pilgrimage of Henry James.* New York, 1925.

Cargill, Oscar. *The Novels of Henry James.* New York, 1961.

Coles, Mervian R. "Form and Meaning in *The Golden Bowl.*" *DA* XXI (1961): 2712.

Crews, Frederick C. *The Tragedy of Manners: Moral Drama in the Later Novels of Henry James.* New Haven, 1957.

Dupee, F.W. *Henry James.* New York, 1951.

Edel, Leon. *Henry James: The Conquest of London.* Philadelphia, 1962.

_____. *Henry James: The Middle Years.* Philadelphia, 1962.

_____. *Henry James: The Untried Years.* Philadelphia, 1953.

_____, ed. *The Ghostly Tales of Henry James.* New Brunswick, New Jersey, 1948.

Gale, Robert L. *The Caught Image: Figurative Language in the Fiction of Henry James.* Chapel Hill, North Carolina, 1964.

Geismar, Maxwell. *Henry James and the Jacobites.* Boston, 1963.

Goldstein, Sally Sears. "A Critical Study of Henry James's *Wings of the Dove, The Ambassadors,* and *The Golden Bowl.*" *DA* XXIV (1964): 5384–85.

Gordon, Caroline. "Mr. Verver, Our National Hero." *SR* LXIII (Winter, 1955): 29–47.

Hofer, Ernest H. "The Realization of Conscience in the Later Henry James." *DA* XXI (1960): 197.

James, Henry. *A Small Boy and Others.* New York, 1913.

_____. *The Golden Bowl.* New York: Evergreen Books, 1959.

Krook, Dorothea. "The Golden Bowl." *Cambridge J* VII (1954): 716–37.

Lebowitz, Naomi. "Henry James and the Moral Imperative of Relationship." *DA* XXIV (1963): 300.

Lubbock, Percy, ed. *The Letters of Henry James.* 2 vols. New York, 1920.

Marks, Robert. *James's Later Novels: An Interpretation.* New York, 1960.

Matthiessen, F.O. *Henry James: The Major Phase.* New York, 1944.

Matthiessen, F.O., and Murdock, Kenneth B. eds. *The Notebooks of Henry James.* New York, 1961.

Ochshorn, M. "Henry James: *The Golden Bowl.*" *New Mexico Q* XXII (1952): 340–42.

Salisbury, Howard E. "Wish-Fulfillment as Moral Crisis in the Fiction of Henry James." *DA* XXIV (1963): 304.

Schroeder, John W. "The Mothers of Henry James." *AL* XXII (January, 1951): 424–43.

Sharp, Corona. *The Confidante in Henry James: Evolution and Moral Value of a Fictive Character.* South Bend, Indiana 1963.

Short, R.W. "The Sentence Structure of Henry James." *AL* XVIII (May, 1946): 71–88.

Silverstein, Henry. "The Utopia of Henry James." *NEQ* XXXV (1962): 458–68.

Spender, Stephen. "A Modern Writer in Search of a Moral Subject." *London Merc* (December, 1934): 128–33.

Ward, Joseph A. *The Imagination of Disaster and Evil in the Fiction of Henry James.* Lincoln, Nebraska, 1961.

Warren, Austin. "Symbolic Imagery in the Later Novels." *Discussions of Henry James.* Ed. Naomi Lebowitz. Boston, 1963.

Wilson, Edmund. "The Ambiguity of Henry James." *The Triple Thinkers.* New York, 1962.

# Index

Adolescence: of Edward Bellamy, 52; of
Thomas More, 21, 23; of William Morris,
46; and utopian personality, 63
Adolescent behavior: of Adolph Hitler, 18; of
the Voice, in *A Modern Utopia* (Wells), 85,
87, 96; of H.G. Wells, 66, 82-83, 96, 99-100,
137n. 10
Adolescent identity crisis: of Thomas More, 22-
23; of utopian personality, 48-49; of H.G.
Wells, 69, 96. *See also* Cultural identity;
Identity; Utopian personality
Adolescent initiation rite: in *A Modern Utopia*
(Wells), 84
Adolescent outlook, rise of: in nineteenth
century England and America, 43
Adolescent psychology: of America, 41, 43; of
fellowship, quest for, 48; of millenarian
fantasy, 17; of Nazi Germany, 18; of
utopian fantasy in Transition period, 56; of
utopian novels in Transition period, 56-57
Aggression. *See* Violence
America: utopianism in, 40-43
Apocalyptic: aspects of Christian fantasy, 115;
dimensions of *The Golden Bowl* (James),
111-17, 121-22; fantasy in *A Modern
Utopia* (Wells), 98-99; masculine battle, in
*The Golden Bowl* (James), 121-22;
violence, in *The Golden Bowl* (James), 110,
114; wish, and idea of progress, 38
Apologies: for utopias, 59-60, 126; for utopias,
in *A Modern Utopia* (Wells), 93-94
Armytage, W.H.G., 39
Artistic commitment, 7, 54
Artistic fantasies, 7-8
Artistic form: and cultural identity, 55; and
cultural wishes, 76; as defense, 2, 7-8, 55,
60-61, 129nn. 1,6; fantasy motivation of, 9-
10; and modern novel, 70-71; subjective
consciousness as, 102, 128; and totality, 11;
and utopian fantasy, 35-36, 44, 54, 62, 82,
102

Audience, response of. *See* Reader's response
Autocracy: infantile, 9; in millenarianism, 18;
in utopianism, 30-31; of Maggie Verver, in
*The Golden Bowl* (James), 108

Bartlett, Edith, 51
Bell, Daniel, 35
Bellamy, Edward, 44-45, 48-54, 57, 66-67, 69,
76, 126, 135nn. 55,57, 136nn. 65,69;
childhood of, 44, 49-51, 53; defense and
fantasy of, 49-51; father of, 50-53, 57; and
fellowship, 51; and feminine rescue in
*Looking Backward,* 51-52, 136n. 69; and
food, 53; hero-worship of, 50; identity
problem of, 51-53; military preoccupation
of, 50-51, 135n. 57; and William Morris, 49,
52, 135n. 57; mother of, 50-52, 57, 136n. 65;
oedipal fantasy of, 53; and orality, 52-53;
religion, rejection of, 54; son of, 49;
totalistic thought of, 51; utopia of, 57;
utopian personality of, 44, 48-49; Victorian
defenses of, 49; and women, 51-52, 136n.
69. Works: *Looking Backward,* 44, 50-53,
136n. 69, 140n. 2; "A Positive Romance,"
51; "The Religion of Solidarity," 51
Bellamy, Paul, 49
Bellamy, Rev. Rufus King, 50
Bergonzi, Bernard, 42, 64, 66
Berneri, Marie, 31, 58, 59, 60
Bible: Book of Daniel, 15; Ecclesiastes, 114
Big brother, 17, 19, 31, 36, 99
Biographical studies, 5
Biographers, of William Morris, 45
Bleich, David, "The Determination of Literary
Value," 130n. 8(top); "Eros and Bellamy,"
136n. 69; *Subjective Criticism,* 129nn. 3,4
Bowman, Sylvia, 50, 136n. 65
*Brave New World* (Huxley), 36
Brome, Vincent, 64, 66, 67
Brother: battle of, in *The Golden Bowl* (James),
122; -figure, in *The Golden Bowl* (James),